THE VOICE OF JACOB

Indiana Studies in Biblical Literature

Herbert Marks and Robert Polzin,
General Editors

THE VOICE OF JACOB

On the Composition of Genesis

LESLIE BRISMAN

INDIANA UNIVERSITY PRESS
BLOOMINGTON & INDIANAPOLIS

Manufactured in the United States of America
Library of Congress Cataloging-in-Publication Data
Brisman, Leslie.
The voice of Jacob : on the composition of Genesis / Leslie Brisman.
p. cm. — (Indiana studies in biblical literature)
Bibliography: p.
1. Bible. O.T. Genesis—Criticism, interpretation, etc.
2. Bible. O.T. Genesis—Authorship. 3. Bible as literature.
4. Documentary hypothesis (Pentateuchal criticism) I. Title.
II. Series.
BS1235.2.B75 1990
222′.116—dc20 89-45194
CIP

1 2 3 4 5 94 93 92 91 90

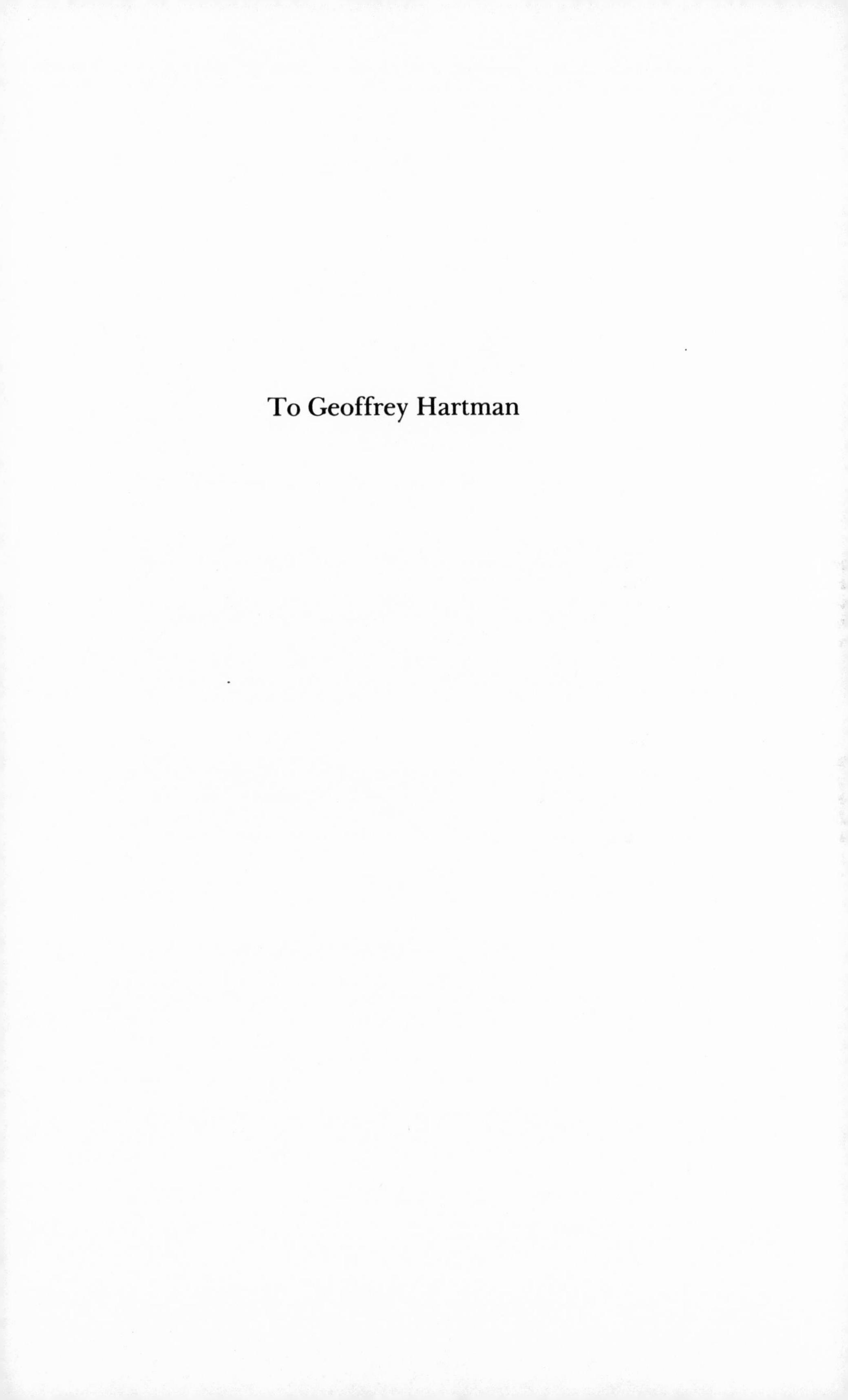

To Geoffrey Hartman

Meaning, perhaps for the first time in narrative literature, was conceived as a process, requiring continual revision.

—Robert Alter, *The Art of Biblical Narrative*

When [these haggadic additions] were written down, it was not disinterested writing, not mere automatic copying. No writer ever writes without some purpose.

—Samuel Sandmel, "The Haggadah Within Scripture"

CONTENTS

INTRODUCTION
THE DOCUMENTARY HYPOTHESIS AND FAMILY ROMANCE

In the King James translation, the Decalogue begins (or almost begins) with the injunction "Thou shalt have no other gods before Me." Although the Hebrew *ʿal pānaî* (as opposed to *lĕpānaî*) clearly means "to my face" rather than "before my time," there is a familiar truth represented in the English "before Me": God's insistence on unrivaled priority of importance seems to require also a denial of antecedents. Christians and Jews may differ about whether the command is the first or the second in the Decalogue, but it is not hard to agree that the added ambiguity of the English accords with a theological absolute: This god tolerates no rivals, mediators, or predecessors. He is *the* original.

Human originality is a more problematic thing. Did any biblical writer "begin at the beginning," or were all forever collecting, revising, transmuting material in more or less complicated relationship to the past? Today we are fascinated by Babylonian and Canaanite analogues or sources for Elohim and Yahweh stories, and modern scholarship routinely questions whether there was an original unity between the Elohim who is to have no others before him and the Yahweh (right before him—in the preceding verse) who spearheads the Exodus. We have come to regard the active worker who forms Adam from the earth in Genesis 2 as a very differently conceived character from the sublimely white-collar deity of chapter 1. The question "Which version of the creation of man is the more original?" may be in part a question about the relative antiquity of the various strands of Pentateuchal narrative, but it mingles easily with the literary question about which seems the more "original" in the sense of the stronger, more imaginative achievement.

From the literary study of the Pentateuch, there has emerged a general consensus about the "originality" of the J author in both the temporal and evaluative senses—at least when a major J author-compiler is distinguished from source-fragments, redactions, or additions "in the school of

J." For most readers who regard J as *an author,* he is the Pentateuchal author most gifted in producing the uncanny, most oblivious of the moral sensibilities and institutional needs that have been thought to mark other Pentateuchal sources. From the classical documentary study of the Pentateuch—i.e., the work of Graf, Wellhausen, and their followers—there emerged a consensus about the antiquity of J in relation to the other sources, a consensus regarded, for a hundred years, as close to fact as the Darwinian hypothesis of natural selection. Even in the flurry of recent challenges to the neatness of the documentary hypothesis, there have hardly been any adherents of the old notion of Hermann Hupfelt that (what we now call) P is the precursor text and groundwork for redactional additions.

Although there was some philological evidence for the relative earliness of J, the Wellhausen hypothesis was advanced less by the rigors of a scientific discipline than by the lure of a single, sweeping idea about the development of the text. Despite subsequent refinements in the history of religion and appreciation of narrative differences, the consensus about the earliness of J remains buttressed by the overwhelming simplicity of the idea of a melancholy progress from the amoral to the moral, from the lawless to the regulated, from the naïve to the partisan, from the unexpurgated to the decorous. In this assumption, the orthodox and the irreverent have stood united: Cynics—with Wellhausen at their lead—pointed to the pristine qualities of J and the loss as we give up his "many-colored robe of fancy" for the somber dress of scribe and priest; looking at the same facts but reading black where others saw white, some pious critics who took over the study of higher criticism pointed to the grand scheme of revelation, the unfolding in time of greater and greater understandings of religious truth.

Let us consider a well-known example of Wellhausen arguing for the priority of J. One of the most shocking and indisputably J verses of the Pentateuch is Exodus 4:24: "On the way, at a rest spot, Yahweh met [Moses] and sought to kill him." Wellhausen assumes that Moses at this point in the narrative is uncircumcised, that he ought to have been, and that Yahweh is more disturbed by this omission than he was by Moses' uncircumcision of the lips. Here is the leader of the people about to take office, and the congressional subcommittee of One uncovers a troublesome flaw that can kill the nomination—strikingly troped as killing the nominee. But just what expectation of circumcision was there? Wellhausen argues that there must have been a tradition of circumcision before marriage, and that J recognized such a practice here as in Genesis 34, the story of Shechem. When Zipporah circumcises her son instead of her husband, throwing the son's foreskin at Moses' genitals and thus symbolically making him a *ḥ^a^tan dāmîm* (bridegroom of blood), she delivers her husband from the wrath of Yahweh—and inaugurates the concept of infant circumcision as a milder substitute for the nasty adult practice.

This much is undoubtedly an impressive interpretation in its own right, and perhaps it gains further weight if we see Wellhausen's reading of the Zipporah story as an etiology of circumcision in line with his reading of the Adam and Eve story as an etiology of human misery. Both J texts get rewritten, in the Priestly accounts of circumcision and creation respectively, as part of "the convulsive efforts of later Judaism to deny that most firmly established of all the lessons of history, that the sons suffer for the sins of the fathers" (*Prolegomena,* II.viii.I.i). Both the narrative act of rereading an obligation and the representation of a central Hebrew ritual as being *about* revision (substituting a milder for a harsher cult practice) make the Exodus 4 passage too sophisticated for Wellhausen to claim that he spots the amoral, folkloric element in unadulterated form. But he holds on to the judgment that we have here a great piece of J narrative, in distinction from the circumcision story of Genesis 17, where the institution of the ritual "throws into the shade and spoils the story out of which it arose" (*Prolegomena,* II.viii.II.3). Wellhausen hails the imaginative triumph of the J story by reading it as revisionary in relationship to a ritual practice, though "original" in relationship to the belated Genesis 17 story.

The most surprising element of Wellhausen's interpretation remains his assumption of a sin of omission on Moses' part: Wellhausen so readily normalizes the sudden declaration of Yahweh's uncanny hostility! Usually such normalization is attributed to a belated, priestly writer or the redactor of the text. Suppose, however, that the J writer gains his power by *unwriting* a more normative account of the circumcision of the son. Suppose, that is, that behind the eerie encounter as we have it lay not the historicity of adult circumcision in Israel but a milder story of the institution of child circumcision at the time of Moses, or even a story like the Binding of Isaac, where God's apparent bloodthirsty will is a fictional "given," necessary for the story's subsequent representation of a truer, kindlier divine nature. We can believe that Wellhausen's supposition about the uncircumcised Moses is more J than the normative, rabbinic readings that Moses failed only in regard to the circumcision (or the hour of circumcision) of his son—but we can do so without accepting the assumption that the story was invented to change, or to reflect a real change, in the practice of circumcision. If Zipporah calls upon Yahweh to "read" the circumcision of her son as the circumcision of Moses, J can call upon us to read the whole episode as a strong quarrel of man (woman) with god—or poet with precursor. The suddenness of Yahweh's attack on Moses would then be not a sign of a story that has been wrested from its introduction, but the story's own best wrestling move against the god of

Stories Old. It would be in line with the argument developed in this book that if we suppose the Priestly account of circumcision in Genesis 17 to be a prevenient text, or if we let it represent the *sort* of text in the context of Mosaic materials that J encountered, then we can better appreciate the uncanny Exodus legend. Zipporah's moral initiative remains as surprising as Abraham's passive obedience to a no less terrible command, but we need no more suppose a history of adult circumcision than a history of child sacrifice in Israel. Zipporah's response—and the fact that only her voice endorses her response—accords with the dramatic attack of Yahweh in the same way that Abraham's silent response suits the Elohist's story of a god who does not take argument for piety. The originality of each author may be both a product of the writer's reworking of a more pallid precursor text and a theme exhibited in the characters and action of the text itself.

If it is incorrect to turn the tables on Wellhausen and to suppose the priority of Genesis 17, or even the priority of a Mosaic legend instituting circumcision in the way that Genesis 17 does, one might in any case suppose the priority of the expression *ḥ^a^tan dāmîm,* a minimal text, perhaps, but a text all the same and not simply a sociological fact. The general point is that the originality of J does not depend on the absence of prevenient Elohistic or Priestly stories and laws, and that creative reworking of a legend and brilliant redactional tinkering may be activities of the same sort of mind—or the very same hand. If I close my books of Higher Criticism and read the Pentateuch itself, the originality of J often seems to me equally or better explained as involved in a swerve from a text like that which we also find preserved in scripture as we have it. For certain stories, therefore, the non-J material might best be appreciated as though it were in fact the scripture as J read it. On the other hand, it is not clear to me that in the evaluative sense of "original" J has a total monopoly on the quality. Some of the passages attributed to E in classical source-criticism are strikingly original, and there are a few P texts that on the basis of literary merit could hardly be passed off as belated, partisan, hack writing. To read the Pentateuch with a sense of its composite structure but without a predisposition toward the particulars of the attributions and datings of the Higher Critics is to confront a complex agon of voices that compete for authority, originality, or what is sometimes represented as "blessing." We may feel that we know the tension to be fictitious since a redactor has assembled pieces of text from strands that do not have single authors or from strands whose authors were not conscious of one another. But actually we know no such thing, at least not while we are engaged in the actual reading of the text, however composite. We may have been repeatedly told such things, but the experience of reading the Pentateuch, and Genesis in particular, is an experience of confronting the copresence of voices that someone has assembled into some sort of uneasy harmony with one another. As soon as we add to the idea of tension the dimension of time—whether we regard sequentiality as relevant to the narrative strands themselves or only to the relation between the strands and a redactor—we introduce the analogies, and perhaps the models, of writer and precursor, man and God. Like Jacob wrestling with the angel, the writers of the various documentary strands make of their strife the quintessentially Israelite experience, where that adjective ambiguously denominates "mastery of" or (to borrow William Blake's term) "incorporeal war with" the God who has none other before him.

If most scholars of biblical studies dismiss the thought of influence or tension between the strands, strands representing single individuals at least one of whom was aware of others, purists of literary analysis scorn the personification of literary strands as themselves authors, persons with anxieties, debts, and wills to power. Yet if we are to pursue the literary study of scripture as anything other than the technical study of the redaction of the text, we do need to hypothesize authorial voices, with personality and intention. Or at least *I* need to do so, for my purpose in this book is to experiment with the thought of a truly literate and literary composition of Genesis. By *literate* I mean to suggest the possibility of one author actually able to read a text of another author, just as the author of Matthew could read the Gospel of Mark (most scholars believe) or the talmudic midrashist could read the text of the Pentateuch. By *literary* I wish to suggest the primacy of intertextual, as opposed to sociological or political, motives for invention. I cannot really hope to restore the dating of the documents as understood by Hupfeld; but I can hope to tilt the course of the literary study of the Bible, however slightly, from form criticism to literary criticism, from typological to agonistic models, from what Northrop Frye has popularized as *the* great code to what I would regard rather as the great competition, or the great competing *codes* of scripture. My immediate desire is to experiment, for once, with the thought of "originals" or originators of Genesis in inspired competition for divine benediction—or readers' allegiance.

In a startling parody of such a competition, Henrik Ibsen offers us, in *Hedda Gabler*, a helpful word of caution. The dreaded competition in the play concerns a professorship in history, valued as a stable source of income; Ibsen does not allow us to romanticize the competition into so noble a thing as a rivalry for a lady's affections or a mutually inspiring effort at great writing. Both Eilert Løvborg, the unconventional, J-like writer, and George Tesman, the priestlike groveler "best at putting other people's papers in order," show themselves to be insufferable egoists who botch both life and work, and we can hardly consider it the moral reformation or spiritual self-transcendence of Tesman when (whether out of guilt or pure addiction to old scraps) he undertakes to piece together and preserve something of the dead Løvborg's work. When he first hears that Løvborg has published a new book, his immediate reaction is, "It must be something he has had lying around from his better days." This careless, dismissive remark has haunted me for years as a representation of what we too often assume in supposing a Pentateuch that has been compiled by George Tesman. Løvborg's published book is new work, not something that has been lying around, and his really great book is very new work, still in manuscript. I cannot deny the basic truth of the Graf-Wellhausen hypothesis that the biblical equivalent of Løvborg's work falls, at some point, into Tesman-like hands. But scholars of the documentary hypothesis have tended to assume that the J stories must be relics of former days, and that the sorters and redactors have sometimes devotedly preserved, sometimes piously rewritten, the old J fragments, never matching their pure inspiration. Even Van Seters, perhaps our most creative proponent of a late J strand, does not return us to an aboriginal P source. He assumes that a more refined J version is a later version, but he still imagines a Tesman rewriting a Løvborg, not a young Løvborg making inspired use of the scraps left by a Tesman.

Although my aim is exegesis, not dramatic fiction, I need, like Ibsen, to flesh out the portraits of two characters—for whom I want names rather than just capital letters so as to keep in mind the idea of individuals rather than anonymous collections of materials from better days. When I started this experiment, I began with four names for four characters whom I expected to identify, more or less, with the traditional J, E, P, and R (redactor). Yet it soon became clear that my business in pursuing the thought of literary composition was to challenge the distinction between *strand* (ancient source) and *redaction* (the actual composition of the text as we know it). I wished to consider the possibility that literary motives, rather than sociological ones, were responsible for the differences between the strands, strands that emerged not as separate records of oral traditions but as text and ur-text, with an inspired author reading, modifying, recasting, or undoing his sources. In short, I wished to consider that Genesis had been composed in something of the way that the history plays of Shakespeare were composed—by one author of distinct personality quoting or revising freely the work of his sometimes noble, sometimes pedestrian predecessors. The analogy may seem particularly frail if we conceive of the strong revisionist in Genesis having the added obligation of being, unlike Shakespeare, the preserver of the very precursor text he is modifying and reshaping, but the analogy may be useful for reminding us of a distinction between what was history (at least familiar, authoritative text) and what is being introduced or rewritten for literary reasons.

My approach led me further into speculation about the literary methods and the psychology of the later author but revealed little about the separate identities or strands that made up the "precursor" text. Indeed, it seemed to me more and more to be the case that however composite in origin, the precursor held—for the revisionist—the status of *a* sacred text and is therefore best thought of as *an* ancestor rather than several. Granted the possibility of such intertextuality, one still must choose between two broad outlines of the history: In one, a character more or less to be identified with the author of the P strand reacted to a composite of the J and E texts; in another, a character more or less to be identified with the author of the J strand reacted to a composite of the E and P texts. The present book is the result of my gradual conviction that, despite more than a century of scholarly work affirming the historicity of the former of these hypotheses, the second has much more to commend it for the understanding of the Bible *as literature.* This book makes no claim to refute, on scholarly grounds, the documentary history as it has come to be generally accepted; my subject is speculation on a possible history of the literary imagination in Genesis—a subject necessarily more involved with fancy than with demonstrable facts, however hard one tries not to betray the philological facts. I realize that I may be naïve in trying to understand how the same person could introduce some of the most bizarre tales and some of the most normative, nationalistic formulas. I realize that I may be wrong in working with some of the documentary strands as though they actually constituted a precursor text, *the* precursor text, available *as text* to a midrashically imaginative revisionist. And I realize how much I endanger the credibility of a few "strong misreadings" by working through the same hypothesis for a multitude of what may be weak, redactional tinkerings. Yet even if these shadows of doubt were to grow into "presences that are not to be put by," I would hold that a student of Genesis might come to a better understanding of the competition of theologies, the agon of literary voices, by supposing—at least for the "interposed ease" of this study's "false surmise"—that a belated author had before him an ur-text corresponding to the work actually preserved in certain fragments of our present text.

I shall call the belated author *Jacob,* after the character in Genesis who is his special hero and representative. To keep in mind the prevenience of the non-Jacobic material, I would like to call its author *Isaac.* But to suggest the association of this precursor with the (currently unpopular) idea of an Elohist, I shall indulge in the solecism of *Eisaac* when I mean the author rather than the character. My Jacob and Eisaac are not exactly J and E, for I am aware of the fiction by which I am substituting E and P texts for a hypothetical ur-text available to J. I will also be attributing more Priestly text to Eisaac than any scholar since Hupfeld has assigned to E, and I will be attributing additional passages and some "redactional misprisions" to Jacob. But concomitant with the reattributions, a certain consistency in what Wallace Stevens calls the "motive for metaphor" will typify these authorial characters.

In borrowing biblical names for our authors, I would like to borrow also something of the histories of the eponymous heroes, and we might begin with what could be called their birth trauma. Isaac is born of Sarah's desiccated loins and is named (at least as interpreted by Sarah) to suggest not joy or laughter but embarrassment: "God made a joke of me; everyone who hears will laugh at me" (Gen. 21:6). The traumatic event that Eisaac is destined to repeat and represent is the conflation of the sublime and the risible. Isaac is the most sage and serious of the patriarchs and would like to be regarded as "child of the Promise," but his name invariably suggests "playing around," sometimes specifically sexual playing, and is thus a reminder that children are engendered in the loins, not in the mental "conception" or wishful thought of their parents. As a scriptural voice, Eisaac represents the aspiration for dignity and the suppression of the risible, of the all-too-human. From the perspective of the dreaded Jacobic irony, Isaac is an "accident," a quirk of late menopause. But from an Eisaacic context, Isaac's birth is an emblem of timely deliverance from childlessness and therefore from death. Insofar as he is born to Sarah he is a welcome embarrassment, a natural joy, but insofar as he is born to Abraham he is an object of sacerdotal care, and the very sentence announcing his birth proclaims the moment to be a religious occasion: "Sarah bore, to Abraham, a child against his old age [a defense "against" old age or death], on the timely occasion of which God spoke" (21:2). The word I have translated as "timely occasion," rendered in the King James as "set time," is also the Hebrew word for religious holiday. And so it has justly become in Jewish history: The birth of Isaac is the scriptural reading for the first day of the Jewish New Year's holiday, symbolizing the opportunity for rejuvenation that distinguishes this new year from the seasonal one. Isaac's birth trauma, then, is the jolt that turns naturalistic fact into religious occasion. Not himself a priest, he becomes the very essence and emblem of priestly activity, the child bound to or on the altar. Though the episode we call "the binding of Isaac" is of course about the eventual release of Isaac, it is the binding that constitutes Eisaac's human bondage to a religious institution's representation of substitution or the deferment of death. Isaac will go free, but he will go forth ever fixated on the hill of Moriah, ever fixed in our consciousnesses as the emblem of the sacerdotal. It is small wonder that the text represents Sarah as dying immediately after; the natural child dies in Isaac as though it had gone up in smoke, and the loss of the natural child is all that his mother can bear. Henceforth no youthful Form of Love, Isaac will be married off when the servant who is his alter ego substitutes filial piety for sexual desire.

One of the indications of the enormous pathos surrounding the sacrifice of the natural man to the "Eisaac" idea is that, from Isaac's birth to his parents until the death of his father, Isaac speaks but one line: "Here is the fire and the wood, but where is the lamb for sacrifice?" This is a deeply moving moment, regardless of whether it is part of an Eisaacic narrative or a Jacobic interpolation. What must strike us, at the start of a quest for the Eisaacic line in Genesis, is the irony implicit in the idea of "Isaac's lines" (what he says in the Eisaacic script): to Isaac the character belong the most awesome silences, for his destiny has been written before his birth. To Eisaac the writer likewise belong the most awesome silences, for his piety translates composition into transmission, telling into retelling. What he "made up" he made in the image of what he received, always effacing selfhood. Himself "already written," as it were, Eisaac becomes the symbol of the preservative character of religious tradition. The tradition may help preserve us from the terrors of facing ourselves as isolate, cut off before and aft, but in preserving our sense of continuity with generations past and to come, it preserves also itself. The Eisaacic text is carved in the altar stones, always already inscribed.

Jacob's birth is attended by a trauma of a different order. Born to succeed—at least in the sense of being second in the patriarchal roster—Eisaac's characteristic anxiety is that he might trespass beyond the limits of prescribed secondariness. But Jacob's birth is attended by no annunciation of comparable status, and Jacob's characteristic anxiety is that a less desirable secondariness might prove his lot in life. Where Isaac's birth is announced by an angel, Jacob's has to be specially entreatied of a God who may have slumbered. Where Isaac is born sole child of his mother, and is specially welcomed into the faith with the first party in scripture, Jacob has to share his birth with his brother, and his childhood is completely elided from the biblical account. We can fill in the childhood traumas, however, by voicing for the child a midwife's observation raised beyond natural taunt to nightmarishly internal threat: "Jacob, you are a heel, a hanger-on, an afterbirth or after-word, a secondary talent and no original!" It is against this that Jacob asserts himself as *the original,* patron of writers who achieve that mastery we call having one's own voice. Crucial to this idea of Jacob is the distinction between the prophecy about Isaac, made to Abraham, and the prophecy about Jacob, made to Rebecca alone. She has to solicit God for some word of comfort concerning the painful struggle in her womb, and God responds, as I understand it, to Rebecca—not to Rebecca and Isaac. What is known to her alone, and absorbed in the very marrow of Jacob's bones, is not only the final outcome but the ferocity of the struggle for priority in matters that count. We can hear, in that prophecy of the two brothers struggling for preeminence, some of the fierce nationalism that so distinguishes the agonistic

God of Jacob from the more dignified and distant universal ruler his father worshiped.

It is convenient to represent the theological differences between Eisaac and Jacob by giving the god each worships a separate name. We can call Eisaac's god *Elohim,* thus transliterating the general name by which he is called. More often we can just say "God." But Jacob's god has a proper name as well as some other, more human attributes or appearances. This is not a scholarly book, in step with Anglo-American successors to the justly revered Germanic tradition, and so to avoid the scholarly "Yahweh," and to suggest something of the familiarity bordering on sacrilege that is associated with the appearance and naming of the deity in Jacobic narratives, I shall coin the transliteration *Yava.* If the coinage in Hebrew really belongs to Jacob, a Jacob who can read and react to Eisaac's text and Eisaac's god, we will not be surprised to find Jacob occasionally referring to Elohim; Jacob can talk about and name the Eisaacic god. The name *Yava,* on the other hand, is totally absent from the Eisaacic text. Perhaps we can say that the development of the concept of Yava from its Eisaacic predecessor represents, in brief, the development of the voice of Jacob.

INTRODUCTION II
A MIDRASH ON THE FIRST INTRODUCTION

How is it that the standard form of Jewish benediction contains a grammatical inconsistency, beginning in second person and concluding in third? For example, before study one says, "Blessed be you, Lord, our God, King of the universe, who has sanctified us with his commandments [rather than 'who have sanctified us with your commandments'] and ordained for us the study of Torah."

The Great Assembly was once considering the question of *maṭbeaʿ tĕpillâ* (the "coin" or "gold standard" of true prayer). A spokesman for the House of Eisaac explained, "To show our reverence for the Holy One, Blessed be He, whose transcendence is beyond our comprehension and whose Presence is not subject to our will, we recite 'Blessed be He'. . . ." But the School of Jacob insisted, "We are not praying unless we confront God head-on, face to face: 'Blessed be You.'" Reb Dactor, leader of the assembly, appealed to his colleagues to no avail to resolve this dispute and get on with the study of the substance of the benedictions, what follows their introductory formula. Finally, he lifted his arms toward heaven, and appealed to the Almighty—or to the good will of those assembled who would overhear his prayer: "May the Master of the Universe give us the wisdom to resolve this dispute and continue with the study of his commandments!"

When he reached the words "*his* commandments," the walls of the assembly house trembled, the heavens darkened, and a still small voice proclaimed: "Let them say, 'who has sanctified us with his commandments.'"

The leader of the School of Jacob stood up and protested, "We do not decide matters of law on the basis of a heavenly voice!" Whereupon the Heavenly Voice, speaking more quietly still than she had before, sighed and answered: "What I have uttered I have uttered, and it cannot be revoked. Let them say, 'who has sanctified us with his commandments,' but precede this formula with 'Blessed be you.' If I have given Eisaac the priority of judgment, you may give Jacob's view the priority of place in the benediction formula. So shall the second ever be the first."

This compromise the rabbis elevated into its own form of blessedness: Whoever hears, in the benediction formula, the voice of the House of Eisaac and the voice of the House of Jacob, calls into being the voice of the Divine Presence herself.

THE VOICE OF JACOB

·1·

SECOND THOUGHTS

> Seat worthier of the Gods, as built
> With second thoughts, reforming what was old.
> For what God after better worse would build?
> —Satan in *Paradise Lost*

There is a midrash that between the reprieve on Mount Moriah and the acceptance of the woman brought by his father's servant, Isaac occupied himself with the study of Torah. Genesis itself records nothing of his activity until Isaac is descried by Rebecca where "he had gone out to meditate in the field in the evening" (24:63). I like to picture Isaac meditating over the opening words of Genesis, brooding over the image of God brooding over the vasty deep. Waiting for Eliezer, Isaac had time to wonder at the darkness *ʿal pĕnê tĕhôm* (on the face of the abyss) and how different this absence was from the darkness of death covering the face of his mother. The mother's face, "the purpose of the poem," as Wallace Stevens would come to say, is so far from that "inhuman song," the total transcendence of suffering and conflict, in the hexameral work! If we name *Eisaac* the composer of the opening of Genesis, we can likewise imagine him contemplating ancient Near Eastern myths of creation and purchasing his own sublimity through a number of carefully meditated rejections or silences.

Consider what is not there in Eisaac's account: There is no war in heaven; no assemblage of the gods; no sexual intrigue between competing heavenly creatures; no story of the sacrifice of one god for the good of all or for the good of the lesser creatures on earth; there is no founding of a sacred place; there is no sudden appearance of a physical or emotional vacuum that must be filled; and there seems to be no arbitrariness of will to adulterate the sublimity of creation wholly by verbal fiat. Like Tiamat, who has faded into the impersonal *tĕhôm* or abyss, the entire range of mythological possibility has faded into the silence before *Let there be light!* While we can compare Eisaac's story of creation with the Eridu or others, while we can figure the giant cultural dismissal of the past as a personal repression, we have to admit that neither the silences nor the actual hexameral work suggests anything we could call a vivid wrestling with or quotation of previous sources. Other texts are just not there. If Eisaac's God is single, solemn, and sensible, Eisaac himself seems similarly alone and dignified—a figure of noble, universalist sentiment and of eminent reasonability rather than partisan, eccentric will. Even the blessing of the seventh day seems without link to a specific civilization or body of ritual. We, with our fallen, belated consciousness of ulterior motive, may suppose that a Priestly author has written the Jewish sabbath "back into" an account of creation, but the text itself betrays no such determination. In context, the sabbath seems a pure image of transcendence, of something beyond man that is the aim and end of Creation.

One detail (perhaps an accident) in the transmission of the text can represent the uncanny disinterestedness of this Eisaacic account. We read, at least in the Masoretic text, "God ceased, on the seventh day, from the work over which he labored." Although some have argued that the text is corrupt at this point and ought to read that God ceased from labor at the end of the *sixth* day, we come upon the cessation from labor as something new, something first perceived, "first invented," as it were, on the seventh day. Whether or not this myth has been conceived to justify an already extant practice of sabbatical rest, we come across the passage (perhaps all the more because of the fumbling over words, the repeated phrases that others have attributed to botched editing) as though the creation of the sabbath truly were the most difficult and the most marvelous of the *maʿăśeh bĕrēʾšît,* the "beginning work": ceasing from work is what God "does" on the seventh day, and this event merits a day unto itself. Although the concept of *qĕdûššâ,* of sanctification, is introduced, there is no *ʿal ken,* no unmistakable etiology of a human institution. The seventh day that God blesses may be the sabbath we know (the seventh day in general), but it may also mean just that seventh day, with no reference to human time or human institutions. The voice sanctifying the seventh day remains "wholly other."

Retrospectively, the whole account of Creation (1:1–2:4a) may be seen to have about it just such an "otherness," a grandeur we might represent by Stevens's lines:

> A gold-feathered bird
> Sings in the palm, without human meaning,
> Without human feeling, a foreign song.

The "foreignness" of this song is the distance between God pronouncing his work "good" and Yava deciding that, on second thought, it is not so good for man to be alone. The distance of the first tone from human feeling and human need constitutes its cool sublimity, a sublimity of what Ruskin called the Imagination Contemplative.

Following this extraordinary passage of Eisaacic writing is another, no less grand passage—but in a very different mode of grandeur. I shall call this second voice *Jacobic* in tribute to the wiles, the machinations, the intense involvement with human mistake and human loss that Genesis represents as Jacob's. Jacob's name, from *ʿāqēb* (heel), likewise suggests how much his sense of originality, his struggle for blessing, is a function of a consciousness of coming at the heel of another, which for our purposes can mean at the heel of another text, however composite. I have nothing like definitive or blatant evidence; were it there, the assumption of the antiquity and "originality" of the J strand would not be so widely accepted. But I believe that there is also no definitive philological evidence of the relative antiquity of J, and that in any number of instances the significance of what I shall call Jacobic writing can be better appreciated by supposing a prevenient text, or body of texts, with which Jacob is familiar.

The very first sentence of Jacobic utterance, muddled or complex as it may be, proclaims its antithetical stance: "In the day that Yava God made earth and sky, when there was as yet no plant of the field and no grass of the field had yet grown—for Yava God had not yet watered the earth with rain and there was no man to till the soil—a mist rose from the earth and watered the face of the earth." Although the doubled name of God—or more precisely, the presentation of God with a proper name—has been explained by redactional critics as the product of an editor's mediation, the effect of coming upon the proper name is that of correction: Not so did things occur, over a six-day stretch, by a wholly transcendent and impersonal Elohim; rather, an all-too-human Yava found himself in the midst of things. One might almost say, "in the mist of things," for the effect of this statement of prevenience is to suppose, in opposition to a creation ex deo, that some fructifying process, representative of the order of nature, was already at work. If *Yava* is the first grand antithetical postulate of Jacob, the prevenience of nature is the second. The third, so closely cohering, is the human-centeredness of this version of creation. The stages of primeval creation may be reduced to two: before man and after man. Indeed, the assumption that there could have been no plant or grass *because man was not*—a statement so bizarre, so irrational in itself—makes dramatic sense if seen as a reaction to an orthodoxy about man's belated appearance and subordinate purpose.

It is generally noted that the first account of creation has God creating man and woman at the same time, while the second account represents

Yava God actively forming man, and only man, from the earth. There is no evidence that *wayyîṣer* (he formed) is an older verb than *wayyibrā'* (he created), and the assumption that the abstract creation is more "modern" than the one in which Yava gets his hands dirty seems to be based on a questionable notion of theological progress. Certainly ancient Near Eastern texts provide examples of both forms of creation; there is simply no evidence, and no good reason, to suppose that a civilization is more advanced if its deity is imagined to be distant, transcendent, and manifest in speech rather than in person. One detail that contributes to the sense that the second account is a reaction to the first is the haste with which man is specified as *the* object of creation and actually formed before the world is prepared for him. God forms man from the clay of the earth and then, as it were, holds him in one hand while the other hastens to come up with a garden in which he can be planted. A similar haste governs the creation of animal life: having decided that man should have a mate, Yava quickly forms every sort of living creature and brings them to Adam to be named and assessed. By itself, a text that jumbles the creation of woman as helpmeet and the creation of the animal kingdom seems crude indeed, but as a joke at the expense of the abstract, rational, plan-ahead deity, the Jacobic account betrays a sophistication truly "original." Yava sets about patching things up the way Jacob the character does when he finds himself a second son in want of priority and blessing.

Given the priority and the dignity of the Eisaacic account, Jacob wrestles with it as man wrestles with a divine being, compelling the ephemeral into corporeal form. Nothing is more abstract, more noble, than the Eisaacic creation by verbal fiat and its extension from creation to benediction: "Be fruitful and multiply and fill the earth." In contrast, the Jacobic fiat, "Eat of all the trees of the garden—but not of the tree of knowledge of good and evil," seems peculiarly limited and arbitrary. If, however, Jacob conceives of divine speech as prohibition in order to comment on the nature of Eisaacic theology, then the "primitive" quality of the tale is a function of the sophistication of its misreading: Jacob creatively mistakes Eisaac's God as a deity of arbitrary religious prohibition, or rather he chooses to represent, in the story of first things, the origins of religious consciousness.

Jacob's Yava speaks once to prohibit knowledge of good and evil. He speaks again to declare that his first creation, of a man alone with God's prohibition, is not good. Here, perhaps, is something we can call quotation, though an inverted rather than direct quotation. Eisaac's God had "smiled his work to see," as Blake ironically expressed it, while Jacob's Yava has his doubts. It is not good for man to be alone: This creator does not produce goods one after another but one good, one recall notice. A revisionist at heart, he sees that what he did at first was somewhat flawed and must be corrected. There is a second text (6:1–2) where Jacob seems to be parodying Eisaac's God and where the verbal similarity further supports the sense of reaction to a prevenient text: The sons of God look, as God looks, and see that the daughters of men are good. "Now *that* is something to call good!" Jacob seems to say. Although *irony* is too undiscriminating a term, there is something richly ironic about these misrepresentations of Eisaacic piety: They misread the text but uncover a spirit that may be more the spirit of Eisaacic piety, or what it had become by the time of Jacob, than Eisaac's own hexameral account betrays.

These little allegories of misreading, if they can be called such, are a far cry from allegorical readings per se, readings that take too seriously the story of the fruit tree as the origin of evil. Were such a tale indeed ancient and fundamental, we would expect the Old Testament to be filled with references to it. But the almost total absence of Pentateuchal reference to the Garden of Eden and the story of "the Fall"—even in the Prophets there are no quotations and only a few references to Eden—suggests that Jacob is a belated revisionist playing, in a relatively private way, with material already in some sense canonical.

One more thematic connection between the first Eisaacic and Jacobic passages. As Milton understood when he fussed over the question of the fish (just how does God bring them to be named and subjected to Adam?), both the Eisaacic and Jacobic accounts have a special interest in the question of dominion. Eisaac's God blesses mankind (man and woman) with the prophecy-injunction to be fruitful, to multiply, to fill the land, *and to conquer it,* to hold dominion over the fish of the sea, the birds of the air, and over every creature that creeps on the face of the earth. If it is in this context that all fruit trees are given to man by Eisaac's God, it is similarly in relation to a question of absolute or relative dominion that Jacob's Yava specifies all fruit trees but one or two. For Jacob's subtle serpent, just this complex of questions about dominion and diet starts the fatal conversation. The serpent, ever at the heel, begins with misprision: "Did not God say, 'Do not eat of *all* the trees of the garden'?" He refers to Elohim, Eisaac's God, and if he gets it wrong about eating (or feigns misunderstanding), he is certainly a careful listener when it comes to his own kind. That peculiar, seemingly unnecessary specification of dominion over all creeping things now comes to haunt us in the form of the challenged dominion of God over all—and the challenged dominion of man over creeping things. *Lĕnāḥēš,* to divine, to "serpent," is to be all ear to the Eisaacic God, ready to pick up any hint that might be turned to profit. Such is the wiliness of Jacob.

It is an irony of literary history that Jacob's tales have become in themselves "orthodoxies"—that what once may have been poems of pure imagination have become in turn material for solemn faith. Perhaps nowhere is this more sadly the case than in the story of the Fall—a slight enough tale very much in Jacob's voice, but something of a different order when the revisionist is reborn as St. Paul. Jacob's tales are full of meaning, but it is human, all too human, meaning that catches his wit and his love of language. Did you say *pĕrû ûrbû,* "be fruitful and multiply" (1:28)? And so they do: *wayyit pĕrû,* "they sewed" (3:7), and we might add *wayyarîbû,* "they fought." Literature may be said to begin for Eisaac with metaphor, with something particular and present that suggests something profound and absent. But literature begins for Jacob with irony and with the pun, two forms of competition for a limited literary space. The sublimity of Eisaac's account of first things can be summed up in the profoundly metaphoric statement of the creation of man: "God created man in his own image, in the image of God created he him; male and female created he them" (1:27). Eisaac is the contemplator of such "imagings." The contrasting passage in Jacob's voice is the ironic and punning line of Adam about the creature formed from his flesh: "Now this, at last, is bone of my bone, flesh of my flesh; this thing we'll call wo-man (*'iššâ*) because she was taken from man (*'îš*)." Where Eisaac's metaphor points beyond itself to sage and serious notions of what it means for man to be created in the image of God, Jacob's jest ironically reminds us not only of "biology to the contrary" but of all we know about the relations between the sexes that cannot be encompassed by so neat a paradigm. Both are extraordinary passages, one a supreme Yeatsian "monument of unaging intellect," the other an ever-fresh reminder of Stevens's quip about Eisaacic ideals: "Beauty is momentary in the mind— / The fitful tracing of a portal; / But in the flesh it is immortal."

Eisaac's account of creation ends with what is either a direct statement about or a dignified, quiet allusion to the institution of the sabbath; the passage is solemnly intoned by Jews inaugurating the weekly day of rest. Jacob's first story ends with the institution of marriage, and though millions have heard a cleric solemnize a wedding by quoting, "therefore shall a man leave his father and his mother, and cleave unto his wife," there is something of an old joke available to every bride and groom: The reason a man gets stuck with a wife is that woman was once stuck to man! Jacob's myth represents the desire for lifelong communion, and more particularly the sexual desire, as motivated by an antiquarian interest in the old condition. And ever since, Jacob's Adam, like Luke's Jesus in the story of the Eucharist, is invoked as if to say, "do this in remembrance of me." Whether one regards Jacob's memorable line as representing the origin of sexual desire or as a rationale for domestic loyalty, the wonder of the line is related to the sense that we are sharing not a first ritual but a first domestic joke. Jacob's story is like that of Aristophanes in Plato's

Symposium, where a divided spherical self leaves the halves forever in sexual quest for repair of the cleavage. Such wonderful stories—often in Socrates' own voice—cannot be taken as the philosopher's last systematic word on any subject, but they do preserve things closer to the human heart than any truth of dialectical rhetoric. The myths themselves, ultimately, number among those things.

Wellhausen thought one could detect the antiquity of the Garden of Eden story relative to the date of Genesis 1 because "the fresh early smell of earth meets us on the breeze" (*Prolegomena* II.viii.I). To my nose, a tree of knowledge of good and evil has no smell of the earth, and perhaps smells too much of the moral abstraction Jacob would accuse Eisaac of having; the idea of a second tree, a tree of life, savors of hearty, amoral correction to the garden as Jacob imagines Eisaac might have set it up. On the whole, neither Eisaac nor Jacob is an allegorist, except in this sense that the allegory of misreading emerges as an allegory of life. There is, for example, no reason to suppose that Eisaac or Jacob had a notion of a devil or an archetypal struggle of good and evil. Yet there is a devilish streak in Jacob that leads him to represent himself as both pious diviner and snake, a subtle creature (*ʿārûm*) and an uncoverer of others' nakedness (*ʿêrōm*).

Perhaps it is the very want of theological allegory that led to the Christian supposition of an allegorical representation of Christ and the devil in the figures of man and snake. I believe we are not simply substituting a different set of names but operating in a different literary mode if we say that the curse pronounced upon the serpent represents the eternal struggle of Jacob and Eisaac, with noble Eisaac attacking the head, or desire for priority, that is Jacob's, while Jacob, at the heel, imputes the integrity of the professor-priest's footnotes, his claims to documented legitimacy or divine authorship. The Christian allegorical reading points to a symbol system beyond itself; the allegory of misreading is local and colors rather than consumes Jacob's narratives. Thus the image of Adam and Eve hearing the *voice* of God walking in the cool of the day does not "reduce to" Jacobic fear of the power of Eisaacic creation-by-Word. Nor does the statement of woman's fate, "your desire shall be for your husband, and he will rule over you," refer exclusively to the dominion theme as introduced by Eisaac and exploited by Jacob. The maxim "dust thou art and unto dust shalt thou return" takes some of its meaning from our memory of the story that man was formed directly by God from the dust—and some of its meaning from the sense we have that this maxim is a fitting antithesis to Eisaac's "in the image of God created He him." Eisaac's God speaks of a heavenly council only to bury, in the creation of man, any other notion of the image of God: "Let us make man in our image." But Jacob recalls the heavenly council in what seems like an ironic comment on the Eisaacic line: "I see that man has become a little too like one of us, discerning good from evil; and now, lest he reach and partake also from the tree of life . . ." While Yava is thinking about it, we may pause to contemplate the analogous situation of Spenser's Britomart, who is no doubt thinking more about her ideal chastity than her incipient humanity when she reads, "Be bold, be bold"—and then, on the iron door she must take, "Be not too bold!" (*The Faerie Queene,* III.xi.54). Jacob's Adam is shown, as it were, the Eisaacic inscription "Be like, be like" and the Jacobic afterthought "Be not too like!" Lest more fruit from more magic trees make him too like the god in whose image he was created, "one of us" rather than image or shade, Adam is shown the door.

The turn against Eisaac may have been the motive for metaphor, but the result is a passage that transcends its own lightness to leave us with a striking emblem of our exile. In general, we can say that for Eisaac the meaning of each tale is its participation in a scheme of divine providence, and in this sense Eisaac is, perhaps as much as the character Isaac, a type of Christ. It is not correct to say that for Jacob, the center of each narrative is its pathos, its representation of human suffering and human tenderness; neither Eisaac nor Jacob has a monopoly on pathos, though sometimes pathos does seem the prize for which they contend. It may, however, be correct to say that for Jacob the meaning of each tale lies in the representation of difference from Eisaacic notions of piety, sublimity, and decorum. Of such competing meanings is Genesis made.

·2·

DEGENERATIONS

In the introductory volume to his 1900 *Hexateuch . . . Arranged in Its Constituent Documents,* J. Estlin Carpenter points to one of the principles on which the late dating of the P document has been predicated. Many of the events supposedly narrated by P are narrated too briefly. For example,

> the artifice in [Genesis chapter] 5 by which the increase of corruption was indicated, would have been unintelligible to one who was not already prepared for this feature in the story. . . . The writer seems to summarize episodes so familiar as to need no further elaboration. If this impression be just, if (in other words) P writes for those who are already familiar with JE, the later origin of his narrative is confirmed. (Pp. 123–24)

This is not to say that P adds his framework and summary statements to a JE document. Carpenter's documentary hypothesis supposes an independent, well-structured, but rather dull P text, written for people who had JE lore in mind, but not at their literal fingertips. In what follows, I shall be presenting a theory that Jacob had PE material not just in mind but at his fingertips, and that the Jacobic additions reflect "a need for further elaboration" of a text re-presented in the context of these elaborations.

First Murderers

> Adam watching too
> Saw how her dumb breasts at their ripening wept,
> The great pod of her belly swelled and grew,
>
> And saw its water break, and saw, in fear,
> Its quaking muscles in the act of birth,
> Between her legs a pigmy face appear,
> And the first murderer lay upon the earth.
>
> (A. D. Hope, "Imperial Adam")

For both the creation of man and the story of the flood, we have some material in the voice of Jacob for which there is unquestionably another version, whether we believe it to be a parallel, later, or earlier version. Since the Cain and Abel story exists in only one version, a hypothesis of its revisionary character must include some notion of what was there for Jacob to react to. If we put aside the assumption that "P" is a late text composed long after the primeval tales had become common folklore, we can see the marks of at least one obvious tear in a genealogical fabric made to accommodate new narrative material. Chapter 5 of Genesis begins the "book of the generations of Adam" and seems to continue just where the Eisaacic account of the creation of man and woman left off. To fit these pieces together requires no great leap of faith; it requires only that we lay aside our Jacobic notion that Adam must have had other children before Seth. We need to consider the possibility that, like the extrabiblical stories of Lillith, Adam's first wife, the biblical story of Cain and Abel has been inserted as a prehistory very different in spirit from the context it interrupts.

If we regard both the tree of knowledge story and the first fratricide as Jacobic invention (or, more moderately, as Jacobic redaction of myths outside the Eisaacic canon), then the most remarkable feature of the Eisaacic ur-text must be its silence on the subject of pre-Noachic evil. In that bland genealogy, mankind fared reasonably well from Creation to Flood. Adam fathered Seth, who fathered Enosh, who fathered Kenan, and so forth, with insufficient wickedness to warrant dramatic action—or perhaps, simply, with no narrative of dramatic action—until the generation of Noah or his father. Because 5:28 announces the birth of "a son" to Lamech rather than naming the son as object of the verb *wayyôled* (begat), it has been supposed that there is a textual seam here, a break in the old genealogy and the attachment of new material with the introduction of Noah by name in the next verse. The new material relates Noah back to the curse of the ground—to the Jacobic story of Cain. We may hypothesize, therefore, that at just this point Jacob broke the old chain, which once continued with what has now been transposed back to 4:19–23 to help fill in the genealogy from the new ancestor, Cain. Another purpose might also have been served by such a transposition: some scholars of the documentary hypothesis concede that there must have been several J authors, or several layers of authorship in the J school, and that the Cain who founds the city of Enoch must be a different Cain (someone else's Cain) from the one who is exiled to a wanderer's life. Whether Jacob invented or transposed the material about the founding of a city by Cain and the fathering of children symbolic of the pastoral, musical, and metallurgical arts, Jacob has appropriated everything of narrative interest to his own Line of Cain. What are left in the old, Eisaacic Line of Seth are the mere begettings and Enoch's walking with God. Perhaps more startling than the symbolic appropriation of all narrative interest is the idea of relating civilization itself to the consequences of the new first-murder story.

Let us suppose, then, that in the old, Eisaacic account, Lamech was the first murderer, and the same Lamech, after the murder, was comforted with the birth of another son, *Noaḥ* (comfort). In coming up with a far more dramatic and shockingly prevenient tale of murder, Jacob has to fit in the old Lamech material, and he does so by having Lamech himself compare his deed to Cain's—or rather, he compares his actual act of human vengeance to the hypothetical, divine vengeance that was to be taken on the slayer of Cain. Making this harmonizing addition to Lamech's ditty in 4:24, Jacob also adds 4:26, which specifies that at the time of Enosh people began "to call in the name of Yava." The exegetical history of this troublesome line may tell us something about the compositional history of the materials between Adam and Noah. For the medieval rabbis, there could be no benignant meaning to this religious activity; the rabbis share with Eisaac the notion that specific revelation (Exod. 3:14 and 6:2) was required to introduce the name of the Lord and his true cult. Rashi's ingenious misreading has it that *'āz hûḥal liqrō'* means not that "people then began to worship Yava" but that *ḥûlîn*—profane, idolatrous worship—began at this time. His interpretation is reflected in a twentieth-century translation, "Then it was that people began to call idols by the name of the Eternal." If we understand that the Jacobic text means just the reverse, that people then began to worship Yava, we might also understand the force of the line as an antithetical statement: It is against the Rashis, the Eisaacic scholars, the early J-text hypothesizers—against the orthodoxies of both Mosaic religion and the documentary hypothesis—that Jacob brings in what may have been an old tradition of the aboriginal nature of Yava worship. It is thus Jacob himself who tags with Yava worship the two ends of the segment he inserts into the old generational chain. Yava is worshiped by Cain and Abel in their sacrificial cult, and Yava is worshiped with the introduction of Enosh—a name that, by no accident, means "mankind." (In the old, Eisaacic genealogy, Enosh is the father of Kenan [*qynn*], who, perhaps, is the "original" for Jacob's Cain [*qyn*], further associating the Yava worshipers.) We can conceive of both these references to Yava worship as self-styled stamps of legitimacy to the Jacobic additions: To deny the authenticity of the Cain story (the first children as the first worshipers) and the genealogy from Cain ending in the general worship of Yava smacks of sacrilege against Yava himself.

Suppose we assimilate the maximum amount of our current narrative in chapter 4 to the old, Eisaacic account: Adam fathered Seth, who fathered Enosh, who fathered someone now distinguished as Kenan (*qynn*) but once called Cain (*qyn*). This Cain traveled to the land of Nod, east of Eden, and founded a city named after his son, Enoch. A little further down the generational line (whether by one or three generations originally does not matter) Lamech gives birth to three sons, one of whom (with a name like Abel—*ybl* in place of *hbl*) is the father of shepherds and one of whom brings the more dubious benefits of metalwork. (The compound name Tubal-Cain may indicate a later attempt to connect this founder with another version of the first misuser of weapons.) In the Eisaacic account I am hypothesizing, it appears almost incidental that this same Lamech is the first murderer.

If even such an enriched genealogy does not look very interesting, we are judging it, as perhaps we should, with Jacobic eyes. The conflict between sedentary and nomadic life, the origins of civilization and the arts, the beginnings of vengeance, that social form of entropy—all these are here no more than topics for the creative imagination. It makes no sense, no literary sense, that several hundred years after the encoding of a tale of fratricide among the children of Adam someone should write a genealogy of the children of Lamech in which there are three brothers, one a half-brother, each associated with powerful symbols of the arts and ways of life, with no story, no outcome to this "setup." It makes less sense that the same hand responsible for the Cain and Abel story should produce the dry tidbits of information in the so-called J genealogy. But given such materials as the Lamech family tree, especially given some special status to such genealogical notes, we can suppose the story of the first murder being reinvented in more dramatic form. The Cain and Abel story is the new invention.

Jacob reimagines Tubal-Cain or Kenan as an earlier spokesman for civilized life—Cain the farmer. Better to represent the conflict between ways of life as a conflict between brothers, Jacob brackets the symbolic musician and gives us just one brother of stable homestead, perhaps ironically adulterating his name *ybl* (Jabel) to *hbl* (Abel), to suggest punningly that he will prove the *hebel* (vanity, breath), the sanctimonious but incorporeal brother. Upon the shoulders of the other brother will lie the burden of association with Nod (a place-name without etymology in the Eisaacic account but associated with wandering, with Cain's assumption of Abel's nomadic ways, in the tale Jacob tells). More important, it will fall on the shoulders of this Cain to come up with a more interesting murder than that attributed by Eisaac to father Lamech. Although I put this frivolously, I mean to suggest, on the contrary, that there is a motive somewhat like piety to the revisionist teller of tales. If anyone, it is the fantastic sociological theorists about ancient Canaan who should bear the charge of irreverence in supposing that a group need (such as giving the Kenites a prehistory) rather than a literary need is the "motive for metaphor." The piety of the revisionist, or what is near-piety, is the faith that there must be a better story to tell. Eisaac, as preserver of the story of Lamech, has uncovered the nakedness of his imagination; Jacob, walking backwards, performs the compositional equivalent of the good deed of Noah's sons.

We owe it to Jacob, however, to pause over the little bit of verse attributed to Lamech the character in the text and attributable, or attributable in part, to an ur-J text. It is certainly in archaic form:

> Adah and Tzilah, hear my voice;
> Wives of Lamech, give ear to my saying:
> For I have slain a man because of my wound,
> A boy, for striking me.
> For Cain would be avenged seven-fold,
> But Lamech, seventy-seven-fold.
>
> (4:23–24)

It is possible that no comparison is intended, and that Lamech is simply announcing, in the doubled form of ordinary Hebrew verse, that he has taken vengeance, and (in the restatement or parallel verse) that since an affront to one is an affront to all, his ancestor Cain is likewise many times avenged. But several commentators have pointed out that because it is unusual and awkward to have two lines begin with *kî* (for), there is reason to suppose that the reference to Cain has been added on. If this is true, the poem in short form could be Eisaacic material, briefly announcing the first murder, while Jacob could be relating Lamech's act of vengeance to his new story of Cain. In any event, Jacob may have come upon the Lamech ditty as an abbreviated and inadequate account of first murder, and presented in the Cain and Abel story his strong-minded reaction.

The tale begins, in Jacobic fashion, with a fantastic etymology, something we can call a pun if we suppose that the meaning attributed to the name is competing for the space occupied by the name in its facticity—the name as "given." Cain's name probably had something to do with spears or metalwork—at least the Eisaacic Kenan's name might be so derived. In Jacobic, reworked metal, Eve says, *qānîtî ʾîš ʾet-YHWH,* "I have acquired a man of (by? from? in rivalry to?) Yava." In Eisaacic spirit, some translations give "with the help of God," but this wording obscures the Jacobic sense of rivalry. What she rivals is not simply the Jacobic story in which woman is created from man but the Eisaacic Lamech-poem. *Qinyān,* legitimate acquisition, birth, replaces *nĕqāmâ,* vengeance or death. The use of the object particle *ʾet* to mean "with" may not be uncommon, but in the Eisaacic genealogies it may be especially associated with Enoch, the character about whom it is said, *wayyithallēk ʾet hāʾĕlōhîm*—he "walked [with] God."

Both the Lamech lines and the verses about Enoch are characterized by a peculiar precipitousness: We only hear about the wrong Lamech suffered when he announces that he has taken abundant revenge. The peculiar description of Enoch—he walked with God and *was not*—likewise hastens the end by making the walk with God that is death look just like the walking with God that is an expression for leading a godly life. The cursory nature of these biographies may be itself the most significant feature in terms of incentive for a more leisurely story. Just as we do not need to suppose that a J story was once matched by an E version of the same events, we do not need to suppose that a particular story originated as a counter to an equally elaborate tale; the course of postbiblical midrash suggests that it is often the very brevity of a story, the feeling that too much has been omitted, that inspires new invention. From a reading of the Eisaacic materials, Jacob's midrash about the first murder may translate peculiar haste into the form of a judgment we are not given time to understand; We hear that Yava prefers the offering of Abel to that of Cain before we are told anything about the brothers' feelings about God or each other. But once Cain sulks, Yava is represented doing something we have not previously seen—indeed, something we may never again see in quite the same, leisurely way in Genesis: He presents Cain with a choice, a temporal lag in which to "premeditate."

The unusual nature of this moment may be a cause, rather than an effect, of the textual problem in Yava's speech. As the Masoretic text stands, there seems to be a feminine noun, *ḥaṭṭāʾt* (sin) as subject for a masculine verb, *rōbēṣ* (crouches). Some have proposed to read the line as though *rōbēṣ* were not a verb at all but the name of a demon who personifies sin. God says to Cain, "What are you angry about? Why are you sulking? If your will [toward me] is good, exaltation will follow; but if your will [toward me and toward your brother] is ill, the demon Robetz crouches at the door of sin. He wants to get you, but you can still master him!" (4:6–7). But it is not like Jacob to revive the pre-Eisaacic demonology, and it is certainly not characteristic of Jacob elsewhere to pose a moral alternative with this degree of clarity about the forces of good and evil. Most unlikely—given how pointed is the similar statement of frustrated desire in 3:16, "Your desire will be for your husband, but he will have the mastery over you"—is the "waste" of the trope of desire on an abstraction like "Sin." I suppose, instead, that Jacob distinguishes desire for amicable relations from the fact of lordship and apportions the two states between Abel and Cain: "*His* [Abel's] desire will be for you, but you will have the upper hand over him." Thus Jacob's Yava sounds less like a Puritan preacher and more like a wily serpent. The advice is still moral, rather than immoral, but it sounds something like amoral, practical advice, the equivalent of the colloquial "lie low!" This is precisely the meaning of the first three words, if we understand them as an imperative to Cain: *lappetaḥ ḥaṭṭā' tirbōṣ* (assuming a transposition of the letter *tav*) or, as is, *lappetaḥ ḥaṭṭā't, ribōṣ!*—crouch at the door of sin, keep your anger at bay, your might half-slumbering. If this is, alas, just what Cain finds he cannot do, it is no accident that the word expressing Cain's violence against Abel is *wayyāqām* ("he rose," "he rose up against"—the antithesis of lying low—with a pun on the word for revenge). Cain's punishment for his act of violence against Abel—and for forcing the earth to open her mouth in pain—is alienation from the earth, or more precisely, the curse nevermore to know earth's "might": Agriculture will henceforth be difficult because in breaking the natural tie of "desire" between the brothers, Cain has broken the tie to nature itself; exercising his might where he had only to curb it, he is exorcized from the life-giving might of the earth.

The law "Thou shalt not kill" is not at this point engraved in stone. That is, this essential moral prohibition does not belong to the body of Eisaacic material that Jacob found already there in the story of pre-Noachic times. We hear this authoritative pronouncement through the voice of Jacob, as the present cry of Abel's blood. Here indeed is a fundamental principle, a moral prerogative expressed as a firstborn's or lion's share of divine authority. The remarkable thing is that Jacob has made it his own. When Yava inscribes a sign on Cain's brow, he appears to inaugurate the world of signs—and the world of vengeance—that belongs to Lamech and the decadent sons of Adam; but the cry of the blood of Abel precedes the inscription and represents, as it were, the last cries of a vanished era. From Jacob's perspective, the old time is the time of speech as presence, the time of easy conversation between man and God or man and brother; the good old time was the time when the voice of God could be heard in the garden before that voice or the voice of Abel's blood meant death. Jacob has succeeded in reversing the priority of Eisaacic creation-by-Word over Jacobic insertions and inscriptions. Reading Genesis as Jacob gives it to us, we are rapt in the illusion of an aboriginal Jacobic voice that is thwarted by the coming of Eisaacic writing—and death.

Starting Over

Chapter 5 of Genesis begins with Eisaacic sublimity: "This is the book of the generations of man: In the day God created man in his image, male and female created he them." Although the "book of generations" may literally refer to the roll call that follows, there is a dignity to the opening verses that suggests that these words account for the whole story: If one fully appreciates the meaning of being created in the image of God, one has, as it were, all of Torah—the entire "book of the generations of man."

Most of the remainder of chapter 5 represents Eisaac at his most pedestrian, recording bits of genealogy as though the mere mention of great numbers of years were enough to impress us with the glory of the past. Such passages remind us of the virtues of the old Hupfeld hypothesis of an earlier groundwork in relation to which the beautiful, sophisticated E stories are secondary accretion. Whether we regard the ur-text as single or composite, there seems to be a Jacobic insertion in 5:29, a fabricated etymology of Noah's name that helps tie the old Noah story to the Jacobic Adam and Eve tale. But it is just one moment. In contrast, perhaps in irreverent, witty contrast with the stuff of chapter 5, Jacob pictures God, in chapter 6, deciding to limit man's life span to a hundred and twenty years. In the story of Babel and in the punning use of the name Shem (name), Jacob will have much else to say about the Eisaacic mode of doing homage to the old heroes; but chapter 6 opens with a truly surprising fragment from the old scrapbook. It is as though Jacob turned back the scroll of history to an earlier column than Eisaac dared acknowledge, and glimpsed there, in the prehistory of the faith, a little bit of the pantheon before the creation of the world by an Elohim single in himself and singularly interested in the story of man. "When man started spawning and there were lots of women around, the sons of God took a look and saw that the daughters of men were most appealing, and took as many as they pleased." I see in this verse not simply an alternate tradition of parallel antiquity but a specifically antithetical statement: "That tedious genealogy of yours, Eisaac—that's your idea of calling up the past; this is mine!" There is no reason that we cannot hear in the "sons of Elohim" a reference to an archaic theology at the same time that we acknowledge such a pantheon to be not prehistoric but post-Eisaacic, written in ironic contrast. That is, whether Jacob as redactor "imports" ancient material or whether Jacob as writer invents new material, the effect in relation to the established Eisaacic material is the same. The very idea of "sons of God" who sire children on the daughters of men mocks the sacred imagery of man created in the image of God—the most dignified of precepts to which the Eisaacic opening of chapter 5 recurred.

Different from the parodic component, yet coextensive with it, is what might be called the allegorical significance of the episode as it relates to the conflict of voices in scripture. Eisaac has a strange abhorrence of the mingled thing—a temperamental, or rather a theological, bias against mixtures, manifest in prohibitions against mixtures of blood in intermarriage and perhaps related to ritual prohibitions against mixtures of fabric or crop or against eating the flesh of animals that can't make up their minds if they creep or swim. Jacob, on the other hand, is fascinated with the mingled thing, as is unforgettably represented in the tale of the patriarch Jacob tampering with the reproduction of mottled flocks in Genesis 30. One might call Eisaacic the conventional documentary hypothesis with its notion of separate strands that have been belatedly, redactionally mixed; the Jacobic theory would be that composition and redaction are themselves mingled things. Instead of assuming that in the old days there were pure strands—a J and an E collection, for example—which then were botched by editorial assimilation, the Jacobic theory finds inspiration in the opportunity to mingle new writing with a prevenient strand. Like a son of God, the Jacobic writer sees how fair are the daughters of the earth, and couples with them. Some may regard this as rape, as irreverent handling of the "given"; but the results may be giant offspring.

We do not need to believe such an allegory of composition in order to note that something new in the way of minglings does indeed follow in the text. Up until this point, major Eisaacic and Jacobic passages followed one another or competed with a relatively low level of tension between them. But at this point, the story of Noah introduces a truly mingled tale, one in which pieces of Jacobic and Eisaacic narrative have been more problematically intertwined. If one holds the customary documentary hypothesis of a belated P version that has been redacted together with a J text, one has to account for the unusually high degree of repetition—the salvaging of both versions—and the redactional obliviousness to contradictions; if one is to hold a vision of Jacobic revision, one still has to account for what seems to be a high degree of repetition and distinction without a difference. Let us attempt such accounting.

Eisaac's Noah story begins in 6:9 with a proper sequence to the "generations of Adam":

> These are the generations of Noah: Noah was a just man and perfect in his generation, and Noah walked with God. And Noah begat three sons, Shem, Ham, and Japeth. The earth also was corrupt before God; and the earth was filled with violence. And God looked upon the earth, and behold, it was corrupt; for all flesh had corrupted his way upon the earth.

The dignity of this passage is well caught in the King James translation, despite the inadequacy of "generations" for *tôlĕdōt.* That is, one would do more violence to the text in translating, "This is the story of Noah" and thus losing the parallelism to "This is the book of the generations of Adam." The "generations" of Noah stand up to the "degenerations" of his age. Whatever we say about the dignity of the narrative as a whole, we must clarify it as a dignity of Eisaac's God. He sees the earth with the distance and solemnity of Imagination Contemplative; indeed, *wayyarĕ' 'ĕlōhîm 'et-hā'āreṣ wĕhinnēh nišḥātâ* (God saw that the land was corrupt) echoes and reverses God's observation of Creation in the Eisaacic account: God saw that it was good.

Jacob picks up the story with Yava's human, all-too-human, sorrow that Creation has gone awry:

> Yava saw that man's evil filled the land and that his instinct for evil was unthwarted day in and day out. Yava regretted that he had made man; he felt heartsick. Yava said: "I will blot out the man whom I created from the face of the earth: From man to beast, unto crawling things and birds of the sky [will I destroy] because I regret having made them." (6:5–7)

Some redactional critics, noting that Yava uses the word *bārā'tî* instead of *yāṣartî* for "created," attribute the presence of a P word to a redactor's harmonizations. But if this speech represents a Jacobic reaction to an Eisaacic Creation, it is altogether appropriate that we should find an Eisaacic tag-word in Yava's speech, and the same is true of the phrases including all of animal creation: Jacob, revising Eisaac, represents Yava undoing the work of Elohim. It is no flippant or merely verbal "undoing." Yava sorrows over the evil that Eisaac so casually mentions as having been introduced about this time; Jacob's Yava reacts with Imagination Penetrative to match Eisaac's Contemplative sobriety. There is also subtle humor here in the gross dismissal of human nature and in the play on *wayyin-nāḥem,* God "regretted," using the same root from which Noah's name is said to derive. (Noah's name would have to be Nachum or Menachem in order to come from the root *nḥm* and imply "comfort" or "reprieve." But Jacob is interested only in *imaginatively* correct philology, and the idea that Yava "Noah'd" creation, both regretting and ultimately pitying and granting reprieve, turns etymology into synecdochal truth.) By the end of the story, the more dramatic revision of the will—in both Eisaac's and Jacob's account—will be the divine decision never again so to interrupt the course of nature. It is especially against this larger drama that we must read Jacob's penetrative touch when he has Yava regret the creation of man. The story itself will move from regret to comfort, the other meaning of the root *nḥm,* but Jacob does not hesitate to depict a benevolent deity sickened at heart, saddened by what he sees. This choice is very different from Eisaac's verb of mental action for the deity, *zkr* (God "remembered" Noah, 8:1), for God's memory is a sign of his immortality, his bondage to the covenant.

For Eisaac, the most important theme of the Noah story is the covenant that not only emerges from the flood but preludes it. In declaring "But with thee will I establish my covenant" (6:18), God not only anticipates his pledge never to destroy mankind by water but extends the covenant to include Noah's obedient preparations, on the one hand, and God's salvific care, on the other. If we believe the redactional critics who say that the present account represents a pasting together of two versions of the story, once wholly separate, we might suppose that the J version of an originally announced covenant has dropped out. But given the way Jacob's Yava is presented in 6:1–8 as making decisions, it seems more likely that the element of prescient paternalism should be just what is at issue. I do not wish to deny that Jacob's Yava takes good care of Noah. On the contrary, one of the most beautiful lines in the story, in which Yava closes the door of the ark for Noah (7:16), is sublimely Jacobic. But this mode of solicitude seems rather a distinction from than a parallel to the Eisaacic, covenantal planning. The hypothesis that Jacob expands upon an Eisaacic text helps the total story as we have it to appear less arbitrary in the matter of which details are presented in Jacob's voice.

If one hypothesizes a redactor mediating the choice of passages, one might imagine that J's account of the construction of the ark was not sufficiently distinctive to warrant separate insertion; it is also possible that J's account of the ark was too much at odds with P's—perhaps because J had God simply present Noah with an ark. But under the theory of revisionary Jacobic activity, we do not have to account for the disappearance of one version of the ark building; there would never have been a J version; such details do not excite the Jacobic imagination. The question of how many animals of each kind enter the ark is more complex.

The standard documentary hypothesis allows for differences of an apparently indifferent nature by supposing at best a pious and at worst a bungling redactor. Faced with a P document in which all the animals come two by two, and a J document in which the clean animals come seven by seven, the redactor includes both. This accounts for 6:20 and 7:15, which are P texts, and 7:2–3, a J text. But there remains the problem of 7:7–9, which seems to have some of the marks of the J author but some of the phrasing and the two-by-two idea of P:

> Noah, his sons and wife and the wives of his sons with him, entered the ark because of the flood waters. From clean animals and from unclean animals and from birds and crawling things—two by two they came to Noah, to the ark, male and female as God commanded Noah.

According to Claus Westermann, "One can see the direction of R's work in 7:7–10 where he has left his strongest impression." But is it an impression of mastery of the materials? How "carefully planned" is this redactor's work? Westermann argues that by creating a "verbal parallel" to verses 13–16, "R has thereby succeeded in giving a dominating role to the entrance into the ark with all the people and the animals." We are asked to believe that R has supplied a piece of the story absent from a J text, or that R has rewritten a piece of J narrative to harmonize better with a piece of P text. But no harmony is made. On the contrary, if this passage comes from the hand of someone independent of J and P, it represents a peculiar indifference to the J account previously given of Yava ordering Noah to take into the ark seven by seven of the clean animals.

The problem is that the passage accords with the verbal usage of P, but we already have a P version of this portion of the narrative, and so the passage must be attributed either to J (with the assumption that the real J has been subsequently adulterated) or to a redactor aware of, in the school of, P. Neither of these theories, however, can account for the inconsistency with the J version of the command to Noah to take seven by seven of the edible animals. If this text has been tampered with, the earlier one (7:2–3) should have been too; if this text is original to a redactor of J and P, he could have tried harder to reconcile J and P rather than ignore the already stated discrepancy. The adulterator or redactor of the text must have been nodding.

If, however, we suppose an Eisaacic text that already contains the two-by-two passage of 7:8 and that of 7:15, then the invention of 7:1–5 can be attributed not to carelessness but to perceptive calculation. If Jacob read an account of the animals that are clean and those that are not entering the ark two by two, he would have found there a distinction without a difference: Why distinguish clean from unclean if not to make something of it? And what Jacob makes of it is precisely the opposite of Eisaac's intention. In the Eisaacic account, man was originally vegetarian and without knowledge of that national deity Yava and his sacrificial cult. God's instructions break off with the injunction to outfit the ark with all manner of food, but it is clear that this food is vegetable food, for both humans and animals. At just this point Jacob breaks in with a further directive to Noah, a directive "sneaked in" as an indulgent parent might sneak in sweets to a child on a diet. "Look, Noah," Yava seems to be saying, "You have been so righteous that you deserve to take seven pairs of the edible animals." The Jacobic causal link here is not between righteousness and salvation but between righteousness and carnivorousness. Hence Yava enjoins Noah to *take* seven pairs of the clean; the two by two for continuity of the species alone could be expected to *come by themselves*.

In suggesting this distinction between the self-motivated animal couples and the additional passengers, I am reproducing a version of a medieval midrashic exegesis. Ramban accounts for the difference between the twos and sevens by supposing that two of every species came of their own accord, "for the preservation of the seed," while Noah had to go out and round up the six additional couples of clean animals who were to be taken aboard for sacrifice and human consumption. What makes this distinction particularly charming is that it ostensibly addresses only the question of the difference in numbers but incidentally accounts for the difference between 6:20, which says the animals will come to Noah, and 7:2, in which Noah is commanded to bring the animals: Those who were destined to be his food had to be hunted down and forcibly brought aboard. I am pointing to a feature characteristic of postbiblical midrash—making the peculiar, the new, seem a product of closer reading—reading that pays more attention to detail. But the same sort of assertion of playful superiority may be implicit in Jacobic material within Genesis itself, and we owe it to Jacob at least to suspend judgment that a discrepancy in details indicates a careless botch. While Jacob's motives may be not so conventionally pious as those of Ramban, we can hear, in such passages of midrashic imagination, a trick of the voice of Genesis itself—Jacobic Genesis.

Very different from these modes of Jewish playfulness is a strain of Protestant commentary that seeks to sustain an Eisaacic religiosity. Here is Gerhard von Rad making sense of the differences between the strands of text:

> It is significant that only immediately before his final entry into the ark did Noah learn of God's plan to destroy mankind by a flood. Of course, only by this communication could the meaning of the ark and its purpose become clear to him. Therefore, Noah completed the entire structure without knowing God's intentions; he had only the command which drove him to blind obedience. But that was just Yahweh's intention—to test Noah. To Noah the command must have seemed strange and incomprehensible. A ship on dry land! That was a test of his obedience and faith. (*Genesis: A Commentary,* p. 120)

For all his attention to the documentary strands, von Rad might have been the author of the book of Hebrews. I find especially remarkable the notion that "the Yahwist here tells of a test of faith." The Elohist tests faith, but for the Yahwist, I believe that a test of faith is as incomprehensible as "faith" itself. To be sure, there is an element of Eisaacic flavor to which von Rad—as well as the authors of the New Testament epistles—responds; but Jacob responds differently, and his elaborations of a tale qualify rather than extend the transcendental quest.

Testing the Weather

Although critics have been uniformly appreciative of the episode in which Noah tests the weather by thrice sending forth a dove, there has been some question about 8:6–7, concerning the raven. The consensus appears to be that the entire episode, including raven and dove, comes from J, and that J himself may have assimilated a three-bird version (such as that in Gilgamesh) with a three-trial version, such as the one we have in 8:8–12. A few, however, have refused to attribute to the hand of J something so dull as the line about the raven. Here is von Rad: "The passage, received from tradition by the Priestly document, is without charm and is inserted into the narrative without proper vividness. Is the meaning of the statement really that the raven did not return to the ark? How different is the Yahwist at this point!" (p. 129). Neither the proposal that P was acquainted with J's dove nor the contrary is particularly attractive. If, however, the story of the dove is written by Jacob in response to the Eisaacic raven, we need not be puzzled either by the inclusion of both birds or by the poignant use of detail only in the second passage. I believe that the Eisaacic text in Jacob's hands already described Noah sending forth the raven, who goes about *yāṣô' wāšôb* (back and forth, hither and yon). The expression, Jacob would have noticed, forms a variant on the description of the abating flood waters, which in verse 3 return *hālôk wāšôb* ("continually," many translations have it, but literally "going forth and returning"). To the Jacobic eye these verses may have appeared a neglected opportunity to make something of the return, especially if the phrase *hālôk wĕḥāsôr* (diminishing further and further) was also part of the Eisaacic text (8:5), calling attention, by its difference, to the *hālôk wāšôb* two verses earlier. In the verses about the dove, *return* becomes a charged concept:

> He sent out the dove to see if the waters abated from the face of the earth. The dove did not find a resting place for the sole of her foot and returned to him, to the ark—for water covered the face of the earth. He put forth his hand and took her in; he brought her to him, to the ark. He abided another seven days and again sent the dove from the ark. The dove returned to him, at evening, and behold—an olive leaf caught in her mouth. Noah knew that the waters had abated from the earth. He abided another seven days and sent the dove. She did not again return to him. (8:8–12)

One sign of the Jacobic intonation is the pun on *mānôaḥ* ("resting place," but with the suggestion of a *nōaḥ* [Noah] place). Another Jacobic element is the care lavished on the dove as though it were Noah and Noah were the benignant deity desirous of his creatures' return but no less interested in seeing them prepared to live their own lives. I mean not to allegorize the incident but rather the reverse—to see in a wholly contained episode emotion and meaning that one would have thought (that Eisaac would have thought) applicable only to divine providence. Noah puts out his hand to take the dove back without that hand's being a symbol of the hand of divine providence. Again, not wishing to expose the bird to daily trials (one might say to Eisaacic trials of faith) Noah waits seven days before sending her out again. Were the sole purpose of the episode to picture Noah looking out for his self-preservation (a Jacobic answer to Eisaac's "God remembered Noah"), the passage could end with the knowledge gained that the flood waters had receded so as to expose the olive for the bird's plucking. Yet the third mission of the dove transcends epistemological purpose. After seven more days Noah sends the dove forth again, and she returns no longer. No statement of what Noah knew follows, though at this point we return to the Eisaacic narration of the end of the flood—a narration that includes God's specific injunction to leave the ark, so that a return to the Eisaacic text is also a retreat from the originality and independence of the Jacobic Noah. The Jacobic insertion ends with a sense of the gap between local and representative history. Children, like birds, grow up and fly off; but this bird is only a bird, and the children of Noah have not yet marked their distance.

Eisaac's account of the flood concludes, in 9:1–17, with the establishment of the covenant whose sign is the rainbow, the bow hung up in the sky to indicate that the ill will between God and man will never again produce such catastrophic results. The massive solemnity of this scene is an extraordinary Eisaacic achievement, and the occasion is marked by the repetition of a line that might be regarded as *the* Eisaacic sublimity, "In the image of God created He them" (9:5). The moral principle of letting no murderers escape human justice, and the ritualistic principle of symbolically pouring off the blood so that the eating of flesh is, as it were, not eating "the life"—these are memorably related to the grander convenantal scheme in which total calamity is put far off. It is against this extraordinary achievement of Imagination Contemplative that Jacob presents an almost whimsical deity turning to a springtime mood: Yava inhales the pleasing aroma of Noah's sacrifice and says to himself, "You know, there's no sense cursing the whole earth because of man; he's just rotten at the core. No, I won't again strike out at all living things." And then, in strongest contrast to the Eisaacic covenant that binds human history to God's word comes this supreme piece of Wordsworthian "natural piety," the binding of day to day without intervention in the succession of the times. These things shall abide all the days of the earth: seedtime and harvest, cold and heat, summer and winter, day and night. There shall be no final "sabbath" (ultimate arrest) to their pleasing alternation.

Dispersions

What follows, by way of aftermath to the story of the flood, is a set of stories about the differentiation of peoples and their dispersion. Both these stories hastily bridge the gap between primeval times and historical times—between the innocence and singleness of Noah, on the one hand, and the multiplicity of nations, the mixed blessing of nationalism, on the other.

The first of these, the story of Noah's drunkenness, may not always have been a tale of dispersion, and its identity as such may be related to questions of intertextuality. Several words in the tale of Noah's drunkenness suggest Jacob's voice, while the dignified account of filial piety bears the mark of Eisaac, in its morality and possibly in its verbal tags (*ʿerwâ* [nakedness] and *śimlâ* [garment] are usually Eisaacic words). To the philological confusion we may add the uncertainty about the identity of the offender against Noah. Was there an old tradition that Noah had three sons, Shem, Japheth, and Canaan? Many have so supposed, arguing that the story of one son who mocks his father's nakedness must have been a story about Canaan, the one who is singled out for punishment. The present introduction of the tale, with Ham the father of Canaan (9:18), represents a redactor's effort to harmonize a J story with the P genealogy of 10:1ff., where Ham makes a third to Shem and Japheth. In one variation of this hypothesis, Canaan has always been Noah's grandchild, the youngest son of the second child Ham, but *bĕnô haqqāṭān* (his little son) originally read or was understood to mean *bēn bĕnô haqqāṭān,* his little grandchild. The sin of the little one easily devolves upon the head of his father since the punishment of the father is the punishment of his progeny anyway.

In so attempting to overcome (or cover over) the difficulties of the text, documentary scholars from Wellhausen on may have positioned themselves, like the pious Shem and Japheth, walking backwards with averted faces. The nakedness they miss is that of Jacob's intention to divert a story of worldwide dispersion into an etiology for the subjugation of the Canaanites. I realize both that this suggestion is not new and that it seems to conflict with my basic premise—that the inspiration of Jacob comes from literary rather than theological or political motivations. But the reshaping of an old tale of filial piety into a story of brotherly subjection may have been just the sort of opportunity to attract Jacob's literary imagination.

If the old wine is the tale of three brothers, the new skin into which it is poured appears to have two pieces: Canaan and Shem. There have been several attempts (summarized in Gordon Wenham's commentary on this passage) to find a historical situation in which descendants of Shem and Japheth are leagued against Canaan, but these miss the point—or what I believe to be the energizing point—of cutting Japheth out of the picture. In the unpointed text, the curse on Canaan may be read, "a servant of servants he will be to his brother" (singular *'āḥîw*), and the poetic (archaic) pronoun *lāmô* in the following two verses may be similarly singular: Canaan will be a slave to *him* (Shem alone). With Jacobic wit, Japheth is discharged as though shot from a cannon; the pun on his name (enlarge, disperse) explodes, and the shrapnel litters the earth—the entire earth, that is, except for the scene of Jacobic scrutiny, where Shem dominates Canaan. Since it makes no sense to suppose that Japheth will dwell in the tents of Shem, we may suppose that the understood pronoun in verse 27 refers to the God of Shem: "May God 'japheth' Japheth, and may [God] dwell in the tents of Shem." From a political vantage, the plurality that counts, the number dear to Jacob, is the number of Semitic tents. But what makes such a passage a literary achievement of Jacobic imagination is the disperser dispersed: the Eisaacic concern with dispersion has itself been dispersed, or at least dispensed with for the duration of this Noachic benediction and curse. Peopling the rest of the world becomes a subsidiary activity, mere background for the essentially Semitic story that follows in the remainder of Genesis. But making the old foreground into background, dispelling the Eisaacic concern, remains central, Jacobic, imaginative activity.

The second postdiluvian story, the story of the tower of Babel (11:1–9), interrupts a long passage of genealogy, 9:28–11:27. This Jacobic turn against Eisaac's list of Shemite names may be represented in the pun on *šēm,* the name of Noah's son from which the Semites are derived; as a common noun it means "name." But it is really the first postdiluvian story, naming the Semites as the privileged group, that seems reworked into a second story, a story in which the human desire for a name looks like a very different thing from God's special selection of one people above all others: "Come," they said, "let us build ourselves a city and a ziggurat whose top will reach the sky. Let us make a name for ourselves lest we be [meaninglessly] dispersed upon the face of the earth." Against the strength of the story of filial piety as such, rather than the indifferent material of the intervening genealogy and its account of the dispersal, Jacob turns to Babel.

Although the effrontery represented in this tale is of a different order than that against Noah, there is a certain thematic similarity in situation and outcome: Over and against Canaan or Ham's assault on the dignity of Noah, Jacob sets a brilliantly absurd attempt at assaulting *the* Father. A sobered Noah retreats to the archaic power of the word and curses his son. Here, a bemused Yava retreats to an archaic pantheon of celestial cohorts: "Yava came down to take a look at the city and ziggurat that these mortals built, and Yava said—'Hmm, We still have here one people, one language, and look what they have managed to do! Why, now nothing they dare to think of will be beyond their power to do! Let's descend and make a mess of their language so that one person won't understand his neighbor.'" Like the other, seminal Jacobic irony when Yava decides to banish man from paradise lest there be no stopping him from becoming immortal too, this story turns on a sense of mock threat to divine power. Retrospectively, we can see the doubling of forbidden trees as a defense against assault, just as, in the tale of Noah's drunkenness, the pious action of two brothers, by the very nature of there being two, defuses or diffuses the energy of assault of the one. All three stories account for disunity or exile as the human condition. Of the three, this one may most clearly represent a religious mistake; but if we attend to the placement of the story and its play with the name *šēm,* we can say as well that the story toys with the idea of religious chosenness.

It is on the occasion of coming across *běnê šēm,* the children of Shem, the "people of name," that the Babel story is introduced, and even the designation of the land of Shinar where the people are said to dwell, *wayyešbû šām* (the same letters as *šēm*) plays with a complex we can represent in English as semen-otics / semiotics / Semitics. *Ûmiššām,* "from thence," or "from Shem," the story goes on, the dispersion proceeds. It proceeds, in 11:10, to tell us again of the generations of Shem and the ancestry of Abraham. With all the rich ironies of this tale, Jacob leaves us with a sense of the babel of nations set over and against the singleness of God's call to Abraham. What is not clear—or what seems to me, rather, to be richly ambiguous—is the question whether the voice of Eisaac emerges from the tale of Babel as a muffled precursor of Jacobic voice (singing the same theological song, as it were, but displaced to the undersong) or as part of the babel of pre-Yava voices. Scholars have often pointed out that in addition to the internal verbal play (*nāblâ,* "let us confuse," as itself a rearrangement of the letters of *nilběnâ,* "let us make bricks"), the playful etymology of *Babel* from a Hebrew root meaning "confusion" displaces a proper Babylonian etymology of the word as "gate of God." Can it be that from the Jacobic standpoint, Eisaacic pieties and Babylonian mythologies are all one? Whether the place is Babel or Beth El, the challenge of a place already occupied is a challenge to Jacob's originality. And if the challenges are not right there, in a text already privileged, they may have to be imported or invented.

·3·

THE CALLS TO ABRAHAM

> The whole elaborate system of redactors and groundworks is unnecessary if it can be shown that the various *writers* who succeeded one another (and who were admittedly also compilers and editors) were directly dependent upon the works of their predecessors and incorporated these works into their own.
>
> —John Van Seters, *Abraham in History and Tradition*

Get You Gone

The question where the story of Abraham properly begins is a question that reflects the literary tensions between Eisaac and Jacob. Medieval Jewish tradition, dividing the five books of Moses into weekly portions, stakes out a beginning with the words "The Lord said to Abram: 'Betake yourself from your land, from your birthplace, from your father's house, to the land I will show you.'" Here is the great divide; here is the beginning of the history of the people. As a second-grader, my son once recapitulated a venerable distinction when he announced that he had solved the problem that had been bothering him about the status of biblical utterance: With the words *lek-lĕkā* (Betake yourself!), he explained, we leave the realm of fable. The story of Noah occupied in his mind the status of those midrashim about Terach, the father of Abram. Biblical or not, these were stories composed for moral instruction, whereas the call to Abram was "history."

In dividing the Bible into chapters and verses, Bishop Langton may not have had just the perspective of the second-grader on fable and history, but he shared the rabbis' proclivity for separating the call to Abram from Abram's family background. The call to Abram becomes chapter 12, verse 1, the new beginning. But the verses about Terach, the father of Abram, are not just tucked into the conclusion of the Noachic history in chapter 11; they are thrust into obscurity, into prehistory, into moral oblivion. That Terach had undertaken a journey to Canaan becomes something not to be remembered, or to be remembered only through the light of midrash: Terach undertook a voyage for material gain, whereas Abram's journey was spiritually inspired. The voice of Jacob, the authorial voice of chapter 12, verses 1–4, 6–9, has been assimilated in popular imagination with the voice of God it describes; the inscription of Eisaac, recording the vain voyagings of Terach in 11:27–32, appears not only to concern an ancestor without "divine vision" but to *be* a text without vision, an uninspired writing.

In suggesting that the Eisaacic lines about Terach are the history while the call to Abraham is the myth, I do not, of course, mean that we should regard the journey of Terach toward Canaan as historical fact and God's call to Abram as a poet's fancy. I mean that *for Jacob* the lines about Terach were history, textual history, while the opportunity to remake this passage into a decisive turning point was an opportunity for a supreme mythmaker.

What did Jacob find? Here are the two passages, 11:31–32 and 12:5 (with the second half of what we know as verse 4 reattached to 5):

> Terach took Abram his son and Lot the son of Haran (his son's son) and Sarai his wife (the wife of Abram his son) and brought them out from Ur Kasdim to go to the land of Canaan; they came to Haran and dwelt there. Terach lived two hundred and five years; Terach died in Haran. Abram took Sarai his wife and Lot, his brother's son, and all the wealth they inherited and all the souls they multiplied in Haran, and they came to the land of Canaan. Abram was seventy-five when he left Haran.

Something of the problem—or of the opportunity—accorded by this passage can be gleaned from the Masoretic misprision that has yielded *wayyēṣ'û 'ittām,* "and they left with them," in place of *wayyōṣē' 'ōtām,* "he brought them out." The scribes or redactors were evidently uncomfortable with the notion that Terach should be such a leader, that he should be spoken of with a phrase that suggests God leading the children of Israel out of Egypt.

Jacob does not tinker with a phrase in such a manner. He interrupts the plodding Eisaacic account and introduces a revelation that wipes away all piddling questions of initiative and place. As readers of both Jacob's invention and his Eisaacic precursor passage, we might indeed have a question when we read, "get you gone from your land." Is Haran Abram's land? And does the further specification of *ûmimmôladtěkā* mean "land where you were born"? Were this so, one might well believe that J knew nothing of what the P text says, that the two were separate strands, and that each has its own notion of Abram's place of origin. But based on usage elsewhere (particularly Leviticus 18:9, 18), we do better to believe that the word means "land of your kindred." Jacob recreates Haran as Abram's place of origin so that this place where his kin now live becomes, as it were, his birthplace. This is important for the story that follows—the story of sending Eliezar back to Haran, to Abraham's kin (24:4); but it is more important, in the immediate context, for making Abram's journey to Canaan seem "original," a setting forth from an original place. The previous wanderings of Terach now serve to remind us that natural origins are always indefinite; our literal fathers can always be traced back to somewhere else. Spiritual origins are mythic origins, with definite time and place. We begin now, with this epiphany—not then, with traces of others.

The old Eisaacic story of Abram continues past the migration to Canaan and past the parting of the ways of Abram and Lot before God reveals himself to Abram. Abram at this point has separated not only from the family as a whole but from the semi-adopted nephew who came with him from Haran. Only now, alone and without an heir, does Abram encounter God and receive the promise that he will not die childless.

To understand the antithetical nature of the Jacobic additions, we need to pay homage to the spirituality of the prevenient text. God speaks "after these things"—after a succession of human efforts that seem to have left our hero alone and without hope. God appears in a dream—or rather, he does not appear; he speaks. And he speaks words of consolation: "Do not fear, Abram, I am a shield to you. Your reward is very great" (15:1). Were the military expedition of chapter 14 part of the Eisaacic text, we might have a different impression of this fear, this shield, and this reward. Indeed, it is possible that the very incongruity of terms in God's address to Abram provoked a later hand to invent or insert the military adventure with Abram as shield, beyond fear, and disdaining reward. Although there is nothing in the events or style to suggest that the insertion is by Jacob, the marks of discontinuity in 15:1 without chapter 14 are marks of Eisaac's hand. The fear is the fear of death, the shield is a shield against barrenness, and the reward (or "hire," so markedly in contrast to hired soldiers or booty from an expedition) is brilliantly, "spiritually" without referent. Although I do not believe that the Hebrew warrants the translation "I am your shield and your very great reward," the statement "your reward is very great" comes as a purely spiritual recognition of Abram. It is a recognition beyond all contract or prior demand by God of Abram and is announced with something of the aura of providence that will be so carefully and deliberately won in the course of the Joseph story.

Tinkering with this encounter, Jacob adds Yava's name and expands Abram's helpless recognition of childlessness into a most Jacobic quarrel with God. Abram now complains, demands, and gets reassurance and a sign. We will need to return to this covenantal scene, but at this point we need to note only that it is part of a twofold assault on the purity of the Eisaacic God's first address to Abram. Jacob rewrites the consequence, and he rewrites the prevenient history. Instead of "fear not, Abram" (15:1), Yava opens his address to Abram with "Get you gone!" (12:1). Yava enters the scene as a more clearly discernible presence whose will is not to be "divined" but heeded, and whose reward is more palpable, more insisted upon. We can contrast *śĕkārĕkā harbēh mĕʾōd,* the Eisaacic declarative that does not mean "*I am* your great reward," with the Jacobic imperative, *hĕyēh bĕrākâ,* which does mean "*be* a blessing!" (12:2). Granted—this phrase warrants decoding into prophetic utterance: "You shall, in time, prove to be so blessed as to become even a referent or name to be evoked in blessing"; but as divine speech, the imperative comes with a directness and emphasis that defies such "decoded" translation and asserts instead a pure "be thou!" Jacob's new poem makes Abram, like a new poet, seem inspired or Yava-driven from the first. In the insistence on priority coupled with a sublime indifference to cause or earned "merit," Jacob's Yava addressing Abram is like Shelley's wild west wind telling the poet, "be thou me!" Chapter 12, verse 1 does not begin the descent into history; it rebegins the poetry of mythic creation.

Take and Begone

We come now to a set of three tales, three versions of a tale, that pose a special problem both to the classic documentary hypothesis and to the theory of Jacob's energetic response to prevenient Eisaacic material. There are three stories about the endangerment of a matriarch: Genesis 12:10–20 and 20 (about Sarah) and 26 (about Rebecca). The majority of biblical scholars who have treated the two stories about Sarah assign the first to J, the second to E, and approach the second as a whitewashed alternative to (or a whitewashing of) the first. One might expect of a three-source theory that the best example of three different versions of one tale would illustrate one each from J, E, and P; but the third version is acknowledged by the documentarians to be all too palpably a J story, and so there is no inherent or "situational" advantage to the three-source documentary theory. I should like to explore the possibility that Genesis 20 is an Eisaacic text to which Jacob has reacted in the creation of two variants, one about Abram in Egypt (Genesis 12) and one about Isaac in Philistia (Genesis 26).

We begin with a story decorous in its morality and dignified in its theology:

> Abraham journeyed from there toward the Negev, and he dwelt between Kadesh and Shur; he lived in Gerar. Abraham said [of] Sarah his wife, "She is my sister." Abimelech, the king of Gerar, sent for and took

> Sarah. God came to Abimelech in a night vision and said to him, "You are to die because of the woman you took; she is [another] man's wife." Now Abimelech had not approached her, and he answered: "Lord, will you slay even a righteous nation? did he not say, 'She is my sister!' and she, even she said, 'He is my brother.' With purity of heart and with clean hands have I done this." God said to him in the dream, "I know that you have done this with purity of heart, and it is I also who have restrained you from sinning against me; that is why I did not let you touch her. And now, return the man's wife; he is a prophet and he will pray for you so you will live. But if you do not return [the woman] know that you will surely die—you and all who are yours!" Abimelech rose in the morning and called all his servants and told them all these things in their ears; the people were very afraid. Abimelech called to Abraham and said to him, "What have you done to us and how have we sinned against you that you should bring upon me and upon my kingdom such a great sin? Deeds which are not to be done you have done with me!" Abimelech [continued], "Of what were you afraid that you should have done this thing?" Abraham answered, "I said [to myself], There is no fear of God in this country; they will kill me because of my wife. Besides, she *is* my sister, the daughter of my father—though not the daughter of my mother; she became my wife. And it happened, when they made me wander from my father's house, I said to her, 'This is the kindness you must do for me: When we come to a new place, say "He is my brother."'" Abimelech took sheep and cattle, slaves and maidservants and gave them to Abraham; he returned Sarah his wife to him. Abimelech said, "Behold my land before you: Dwell where it pleases you." To Sarah he said, "Behold, I have given your brother a thousand pieces of silver; let it be an 'eye-covering' for you and all who are with you, a proof for everyone [of your innocence]." Abraham prayed to God and God healed Abimelech and his wife and his maidservants; they bore children. For Yava had closed the womb of all in Abimelech's household because of the business of Sarah, Abraham's wife. (20:1–18)

At several points in this passage, a decision about just what the text is may depend on a reading of the relationship between Eisaac and Jacob. There is no doubt that Abimelech questions God's judgment in verse 4. Perhaps there is not that much difference between the Masoretic text's *hăgôy gam* and the more normative Hebrew *hăgam gôy* or *hâgam hăgôy*—whatever the wording, the question meant something like "Would you destroy a nation even if it were righteous—i.e., innocently sinning?" or "Would you even destroy a righteous nation?" There seems to be no biblical precedent for *gôy* meaning a single gentile person, but the question could have been (or could have been expected to have been) just *hăgam ṣaddîq tahărōg*—"Would you destroy a righteous man too?" The difficulty about the phrasing here may have helped inspire a Jacobic passage in which the spirit of Abimelech's objection is pursued more relentlessly by Abraham, awake and aware of the destruction God intends to wreak on the people of Sodom: *ha'ap tispeh ṣaddîq ʿim rāšāʿ*—"Will you slay the righteous with the evil?" There indeed the question concerns a people, or at least the possibility of a group of people, whereas in the story of Abimelech the broad stroke of God's retributive justice (in the form of barrenness) introduces possibilities that remain latent. In the context of this story, Abimelech's protest is not much more than a reflex action: "Who, me? I didn't do anything!" But Jacob may have picked up the moral and literary possibilities of a hero who questions the justice of God.

In verse 10, Abimelech asks Abraham either "What did you see?" or (if the Hebrew should be *yārē'tā* in place of *rā'îta*) "What did you fear?" The one suggests Abraham's prophetic power, the other his all-too-human fear of those who do not fear God. The question Abimelech poses to Abraham may be related to the question pursued in the story of the binding of Isaac, a story that takes "fear of God" as a central, positive motivation.

Perhaps more problematic than these variants is Abraham's response to Abimelech, in which he specifies the instructions he gave Sarah. In verse 13 the Masoretic text preserves a grammatical difficulty—they (plural) made me wander—but the subject given is the singular God. The plural *hit'û* could be a scribal error for the singular *hit'â*, but it is also possible that the Eisaacic text originally lacked God as the subject: They took me—people, specifically my father himself, since he (in the Eisaacic text of 11:31) took us from Ur—and set me on a wandering course. Abraham's decision to take matters into his own hands and arrange for the protection of Sarah thus might be related to the absence of a clear injunction from God in the Eisaacic text. A reading of 20:13 might have further impelled Jacob to narrate a version of the wanderings of Abraham in which Abraham receives a specific divine call.

Finally, the last verse of the passage quoted, "For Yava had closed the womb . . ." could be a Jacobic addition and connective tissue between the Eisaacic story of the barrenness in Abimelech's house and the Jacobic story of Sarah conceiving Isaac in 21:1–2.

These minor speculations aside, we need to note the central importance to Eisaac of the theophany to Abimelech: This is the core of the tale, and other events (such as the arrangements made by Abraham with Sarah) are subordinated to the core confrontation. It is in the spirit of Eisaac that we reach the confrontation between God and Abimelech without hearing that Sarah was beautiful or that Abimelech lusted after her. We pause only for the decorous detail that Abimelech had remained technically free from adultery, and then we move immediately to the conversation between Abimelech and God. There seems less danger of violating Sarah than of violating the omniscience of God, but even this threat is averted with dignity. Here, then, is Imagination Contemplative indeed, far above the affairs of the human heart and loins, far as well from the politics of a tyrannical justice. So chaste is the conversation about chastity that honor accrues to Abraham when he is brought into the relationship of king and God in the role of a ritualistic mediator, one whose efficacious prayer will guarantee absolution to the unwitting sinner. Not the restoration of Sarah itself, but Abraham's consequent prayer on behalf of Abimelech will avert the evil decree.

What remains is for Abimelech to converse with Abraham in a tone of like dignity, and this conversation follows its predecessor as morning follows evening in the stately progression of the hexameron. Abraham clears himself by declaring his technical innocence of prevarication ("she is indeed my sister"), an innocence that is commensurate with Abimelech's sexual purity. He also clears himself of "personality"—I made no judgment about your character, Abimelech; I just did not think there was fear of God in *this place.* Purged of the personal, the story stands as an abstract account of moral justice. When the women of Abimelech's household are healed of their barrenness, we can add "poetic justice" to moral justice. The slate is clean.

Too clean for Jacob. Whether or not Abimelech's challenge to God's peremptory decree is the original for the Jacobic story of Abraham's challege of the decree against Sodom, Jacob found more to rewrite in the Abimelech story. The striking chastity of conversation between king and God he reworked into the all-too-particular episode of Abimelech sticking his head out the window and catching Isaac in sexual play with Rebecca (26:8). It is tempting to say that Jacob sports not just with Isaac the character but with Eisaac the precursor, seeing him as he would not wish to be seen. But the major rewriting (12:10–13:1) is beyond such flippancy. Set in Egypt rather than Philistia, the new version gains prominence both in its own right and as a foreshadowing of the bondage in Egypt to come.

In the new setting, Abram has not yet settled in Canaan before famine strikes and the patriarch decides to try his luck in the Egyptian breadbasket. This decision is all the more striking if we see the episode as one of two offshoots of the Eisaacic tale, because the other Jacobic story features a similar famine but a divine injunction not to repeat the trip to Egypt: "Dwell in this land and I will be with you" (26:3). Whether or not the reiterations of the promise of the land in chapter 26 are the work of secondary accretion, Jacob's Isaac is the sort of character who suffers from too great a will to repeat his father's pattern; he is a pious Aeneas indeed and is treated by special poetic justice to a repetition of an Abramic situation that his piety could not have willed. But Jacob's Abram in chapter 12 acts on his own initiative in going to Egypt and quite on his own in persuading Sarai of a plan that, in the Eisaacic text, seemed rather a lie he fell into. Perhaps one could therefore say of the revisions that they help turn the tale into an allegory of misreading: To go from Canaan to Egypt (from divine presence to individual independence) and to go from what Abraham says to what he gets Sarah to say is to turn from inherited tales to innovations, from thoughtless to wily behavior, from solemnity to play. The version in chapter 12 (unlike that in 26) is not in itself humorous or characterized by peculiar elements of human interest; its tone—and therefore its meaning—comes from the contrast to the Eisaacic original, in which the conversation between God and king predominates; now the conversation between Abram and Sarai takes its place: "You know, I'm aware of how attractive you are and how the Egyptians might see you and say, 'She's this guy's wife,' and kill me off while they live it up with you. Come on, say you're my sister and it'll go well for me because of you; why, I'll owe my life to you!" Scholars and translators have underplayed the sense of calculation behind these lines and have shied away from making Abram out to be too Jacobic a character. But this is Jacob speaking through Abram, and it is not surprising to find him playing tricks with patriarchal dignity in the service of his own understanding of "chosenness." In this story, Yava enters, without speaking a word, only to plague Pharaoh and confirm the wisdom of Abram's ploy. Totally missing is the dignified theological conversation between the king and the deity. Equally absent is any hint of that intercessory role for Abram—and the institution of prayer—which we found in the Eisaacic story. Eisaac was careful to assure us that Abimelech did not have a chance to approach Sarah sexually; Jacob, on the other hand, takes care to suggest that this king did precisely that. In place of the dream-conversation with the deity, Jacob's Pharaoh gets to know God the hard way—through his own, private plagues. Using a word for "afflicting" Pharaoh of the same root as the one Eisaac used to describe Abimelech's not "touching" Sarah (20:6), Jacob suggests a very different closeness and knowledge of Yava. Many a commentator has imported into this passage in chapter 12 the information from chapter 20 that Sarah really was Abraham's sister; but the absence of such an explanation is more to the point here. Like the patriarch Jacob—and like that archetypal serpent—Abram remains silent in the face of his accuser, and he is booted out of Egypt with language that scandalously echoes God's call to Abram from Haran. *Qaḥ wālēk,* "take and begone!" Pharaoh says. If this *lēk* is the "get you gone" of God's directive, now repeated in a coarser tone, then the two imperatives together sum up Abram's richly baggaged journey back to Canaan—and the Jacobic version of the Israelites' exodus from Egypt endowed with the jewelry of their Egyptian neighbors. Neither the *ngʿ* of divine/sexual touch nor the *lk* of divine/human imperative is substantial enough evidence on which to pin a strong philological argument for the belatedness of Jacob the writer; but they can stand, synecdochally, for the richness of revisionary possibilities.

Get Signed

The two versions of covenant between God and Abraham repeat an archetypal dialectic between Eisaacic and Jacobic first things. Like the opening chapter of Genesis, with its massive solemnity in setting forth the archetypal sabbath, the covenant narrative in chapter 17 invests the ritual of circumcision with signification so weighty as to make the sign emerge as the signified itself: For Eisaac, circumcision might be said to *be* man's part of the covenant, just as God's part is the promise that Abram, now to be called Abraham, will be the father of many nations. But these terribly important signs or physical representations of covenant are both given metaphysical underpinnings: Abraham's part of the covenant is really that he walk before God, that he be *tamim* (pure, perfect). God's part is that he will be God to Abraham and his posterity.

Perhaps the difficulty in holding on to the pure essence of the covenant may be represented by the mixture of the concrete and abstract in verses 7–8: "I will uphold my covenant between Me and you and your posterity after you throughout their generations—an everlasting covenant: to be God to you and to your seed after you; I will give you and your seed after you the land where you dwell—all the land of Canaan—for an eternal possession; I will be God to them." The specificity of the real estate and the repetition of the promise to be God remind us how linked these ideas were understood to be. That is, we see with too Christian an eye if we regard the land as sign and the status of God as a significance, an ultimate significance. The eternity of that covenant and the eternity of that land possession are inextricable; conversely, *lēʾlōhîm,* if translated "a god to them" rather than "God to them" suggests the specificity, if not the materiality, of a supernatural protector with their special interests in mind. Just as it is impossible to separate these more corporeal concerns from the transcendental notions of being God and of being pure, so it is made to seem impossible to separate these ideas of covenant from the fleshly sign. Verse 11 says, "You shall circumcise the flesh of your foreskins and this will be a covenant sign between me and you." But this verse follows verse 10: "This *is* the covenant you are to observe between me and between you and your posterity after you: to circumcise every male." The purity, the sublimity of the Eisaacic text lies in its anteriority to all Christian—and all Jacobic—notions of the possible distinction between the corporeal and incorporeal elements of covenant.

There is no question of the immense dignity, the weight of solemnity that Abram bears in being "written into" the line of Noah, about whom it is said, "Noah was a just man and *tāmîm* (complete, perfect, pure) in his generation." The injunction to Abram to be *tāmîm* carries with it both the burden of the past and the promise of future glory. But there is some question about the status of the dialogue between God and Abraham regarding the divine means of multiplying Abraham's seed. If the documentary scholars were right in believing chapter 17 to be a belated, P text, then Abraham's plea in 17:18, "If only you would let Ishmael live before you!" would have the aura of an apologist's whitewashing of a rather nasty episode: Here is Abraham, who in chapter 16 seemed so careless about the fate of his first son-to-be, defending that child's rights before God—indeed, that child's right to "stand before God." But I do not believe this plea loses in dignity or importance if we imagine it to antedate the story of Abram leaving the fate of Hagar and her unborn child in Sarai's hands. On the contrary, the coexistence of the two texts makes more sense if we imagine the older tale to be one in which Abraham magnificently defends Ishmael, while the revision casts an ironic eye on the solemnity of the covenantal Abraham. A similar point could be made about the interior murmur of Abraham in verse 17: "Shall a man of a hundred years become a father? Shall Sarah, at ninety, conceive a child?" It adds little to Abraham's dignity to have him repeat a line that Sarah has already made all her own in an old, familiar, J text; but if this doubt on Abraham's part is "original" with him, original to the old Eisaacic text, then there is a curious and characteristic narrative turn when Jacob has Sarah, instead, come right out with the same doubt.

According to a zany but telling midrash about Noah, his being *tāmîm,* or "perfect, complete," refers to his miraculously congenital circumcision. The midrashist may not have consciously regarded as playful the transvaluation of the "complete" or "perfect" physical state from uncircumcision to circumcision, but the midrash reminds us just how closely related ritual and moral perfection were imagined to be. Thus the perfection of Abraham enjoined upon him in 17:1 and his circumcision, enjoined in 17:10–14, are related. So is the moral dimension of the plea, "Oh that Ishmael might live before You!" We would be doing the text a vulgar disservice by interpreting this plea simply as a cover for an older man's fear of impotence. The point is not that an all-too-human motive hides behind a self-effacing gesture, but rather that the piety and humanity are of a piece. Pointing to the son who already is, Abraham expresses the humility of the contingent creature in face of One for whom past and future are equally secure.

Eisaac's Abraham defends himself against the immense spiritual (and sexual) burden with one single, beautiful verbal thrust—not a thrust "at" God, but a gesture representative of both human probity and human initiative. For Jacob the narrator, "the burden of Abraham" is all the greater because Jacob's Abraham bears also the burden of representing a suitable reaction to the Eisaacic covenant text. Perhaps one knows something of the importance of this reaction simply in noting that Jacob's retelling of the covenant story splits the episode into two distinct parts: In

Genesis as we have it, Jacob's uncanny story about the annunciation to Abraham and Sarah follows the Eisaacic annunciation, but the story of the covenant is placed earlier, forming what we know as chapter 15.

Many have noted inconsistencies in chapter 15 that seem to indicate a composite text. There is the Elohist formula, "after these things . . ." followed by *Yava* rather than *Elohim.* There is the nighttime vision to Abram, followed immediately by a daytime ritual that lasts through the sunset. There is a prediction of four hundred years of affliction in Egypt (verse 13), followed by a temporally inconsistent "fourth generation" statement in verse 16. Perhaps most troublesome, there is the famous statement of pure "faith" in verse 6, followed by a demand for a sign in verse 8. Although no simple revisionary hypothesis can instantly rectify all contradictions, the attempt to specify the significance of this text cannot be divorced from some attempt to clarify the interactions between the component strands.

If the dignified Eisaacic covenant of chapter 17 were already written, then the opening of chapter 15 could be understood in terms of a meditation on just such Jacobic belatedness. "Do not fear!" Yava proclaims, "your reward is very great." Reward for what? What has transpired that Abram should be rewarded? We can discount the hypothesis that Abram is being rewarded for his behavior in chapter 14, almost surely a later text. But we cannot discount the hypothesis that Abram is being rewarded for his conduct in chapter 17. Abram reaps the benefit of extended *narrative* life as Jacob reworks the relation between God and faithful servant.

In chapter 17, the covenantal language is mutually conditional: Walk before me—*if* you walk before me as a "perfect" man—then you will be a father of many nations; then I will be God to you and your posterity. This sophisticated, conditional language is foreign and troublesome to Jacob, or comes to seem such out of the necessity for differentiation. I think it is possible that the strangely archaic form of mutual, covenantal binding in chapter 15 represents a reaction to the mode of interdependence in chapter 17. For the starting point in chapter 15, consider a familial model: One parent proposes, "If you will be a dutiful son, then I will be most fatherly to you"; the competing parent counters, "My love, my assurance, is without condition; our bond is very great." In the Eisaacic text, not only God's love but God's being seems conditional: *Lihyôt lĕkā lē'lō-hîm* (to be a god to you, 17:7) leaves up to the future what Jacob reworks into undeniable present. Jacob's *'ănî YHWH* ("I am Yava!" 15:7) replaces the conditional status of God—and sets the stage for replacing the conditional status of Abram's place in "God's heart."

To appreciate how thoroughly Jacobic is the covenant story that follows, one must see Yava's self-proclamation interrupting a supremely Eisaacic moment: Except for the name *Yava,* which I believe to be Jacob's interpolation, the entire passage 15:1–6 is thoroughly Eisaacic in vocabulary and character. This is Eisaacic dream vision, culminated by Eisaacic faith: "Abram believed in [God]; He counted it to him for righteousness." This line, so dear to Saint Paul, seems to spell the essence of an ethereal piety, a faith in the absence of things seen (Heb. 11:1). Noting that there is something strange in the idea that merit should accrue to Abram for his belief in God, Ramban suggests that the pronouns work the other way: Abram believed in God's charitable disposition of Abram's desire for posterity; he (Abram) attributed it to God's righteousness that God should promise numerous descendants to Abram. By itself, especially with the Jacobic *Yava,* the verse makes more sense in Ramban's reading than in that which has become such a standard in Christian tradition. Yet such a reading, which would pit a "Jewish" against a "Christian" interpretation, obscures the extent to which the dichotomy is already embedded in the text in the distinction between Eisaacic and Jacobic notions of "faith." We can represent the contrast by saying that Eisaac is haunted by the memory of Moriah, the memory of a fanatic devotion to a God who is absent, whose will has been inscribed, however legibly or illegibly, on the dream-conscience of an ancestor; Jacob is characterized by the incident at Peniel, by the unforgettable presence of a God who must be wrestled with. Eisaac's God seems absent even when He speaks, and the religious faith of a belated narrator—one who trusts that the God he describes as speaking to Abram really spoke and promised—can be attributed to the character himself. For Jacob, we must change the English word from "faith" to "trust" so as to clarify that it is never the existence but the trustworthiness or benevolence of Yava that Jacob questions.

And question he does! If chapter 15 is a Jacobic takeover of old, Eisaacic material, then the crucial Jacobic turn comes between Eisaac's grand statement of "faith" in 15:6 and Jacob's direct statement of doubt: "Lord! Yava! How am I to know for sure that I will inherit this land?" Eisaac's Abram blindly trusts; Jacob's Abram says, "Show me!" Jacob rewrites the ethereal Eisaacic faith as something far more concrete, and he rewrites the repeatable ritual of circumcision as a covenant event so uncanny that one time is more than enough.

The Covenant between the Carcasses follows aggressively, antithetically, rather than logically, single-mindedly, from the Eisaacic faith in the substance of things unseen. This scene constitutes no "proof" of God's righteousness nor (anthropologists to the contrary) a pledge sealed in blood. This covenant represents, rather, an eerie confrontation with the fearsomeness of Yava, however immediate his response and benevolent his stated purposes. There is a moment in C. S. Lewis's romance *The Lion, the Witch, and the Wardrobe* where the witch Jadis concludes a pact with the lion god-king Aslan that he will die in place of the human kill to which she is entitled. When she asks how she can know that Aslan will keep his promise, Aslan does not argue about his record of trustworthiness, nor does he prick himself and use a drop of his blood to seal an agreement bound by a higher magic. He ROARS, and the witch picks up her skirts and runs away in terror. What we have in Jacob's eerie covenant scene is something like the roar of Yava, or rather the still-small-voice that yet proclaims a supernatural will far beyond our capacity for genial relations with it. If we see in the smoking fire-pot and flaming torch symbols of God's presence and redemptiveness (as in Isaiah 31:9 and 62:1 respectively), we might say that Abram is being given some existential assurance. But more important, if simultaneous, is the sensation of awe rather than comfort as Eisaacic word is made Jacobic flesh.

Literally, Eisaacic circumcision is in the flesh while the Jacobic vision (Jacobic play with the idea of Eisaacic dream vision) leaves no mark behind. But the effect is just the contrary: The stately announcement of the ritual of circumcision contrasts with the bloody Jacobic reality of those carcasses and buzzards. The question of God's signature on his word fades before the dread of his wholly uncanny nature. Whatever the archaic elements in or ur-texts behind the story of the carcasses, we can thus regard this tale as Jacobic response to the too sublimated, too "civilized" Eisaacic etiology of circumcision. The Eisaacic covenant gives religious significance to what must have been (judging by some neighboring peoples) a generationally renewed physical emblem of acculturation. Jacob's story has nothing to do with renewable ritual, but it does offer a variant on the theme of mutuality so much at the heart of the Eisaacic bond. Ostensibly, Yava simply stages and Abram witnesses a night of terror. But both Yava and Abram have parts to play. The model for the Covenant between the Carcasses is an ancient Near Eastern rite performed between two human partners who together invoke supernatural authority to deal with them as they have dealt with the animals they have ritually slaughtered; in walking between the split halves of the carcasses, the treaty partners *act out* the verbal formula "so may it be done to me if I violate the terms of this agreement." Were Eisaac adopting such a treaty for a story of covenant between man and God, we might expect Abram, and Abram alone, to pass between the carcasses; but in Jacob's version, Abram is acolyte, banishing the buzzards, and *Yava* walks between the carcasses. There is no question in this scene of the Eisaacic "faith" of Abram, but there is a Jacobic Yava's response to a Jacobic Abram's request for assurance. More important, there is an extraordinarily Jacobic response to the Eisaacic Abram's faith and the Eisaacic God's "fear not!" The question of the fear of God remains one of the crucial differences in perspective between Eisaac and Jacob—culminating, perhaps, in the story of the *ʿăqēdâ*. We can call it a seminal difference, one important in the generation of "countertexts."

To the best of my knowledge, there is no passage in Exodus that can be regarded as seminal to the composition of an incident in Genesis. Some have supposed that the manifestation of Yava to Abram in the form of a smoking fire-pot and torch suggests the pillar of cloud by day and pillar of fire by night of Exodus 13:21. But since Jacob chose to write *lappîd ʾēš* (flaming torch), not *ʿammûd ʾēš* (pillar of fire); since he chose to write *tannûr ʿāšān* (smoking fire-pot), not *ʿammûd ʿānān* (pillar of cloud), there is no reason to suppose that either an allusion to Exodus or inspiration from Exodus is to be found. The fire-pot and brand are archaic representations of God's presence, not symbols of what is to come. Whether the speeches of God about the sojourn in Egypt were also unknown to Jacob is more questionable.

Might 15:12–15, announcing the Egyptian bondage and redemption, be the work of Jacob himself—or at least a piece of old lore that Jacob chose to interject into his grim scene? These verses are written in the spirit of the Eisaacic vision with which Jacob began in 15:1, and Jacob himself may have interrupted the drama of the carcass ritual for the mysterious effect of one more veil being rent for Abram to see further into history. Upset to discover the interruption of the covenant ritual, some scholars have proposed that a later editor inserted the "content" of the vision; but it seems possible that Jacob himself invented or transposed to this context the description of the sojourn in Egypt. It may have been Jacob's intention, like Shakespeare's when he conceived of the witches' mirror of history in *Macbeth,* to mix with the dark proceedings of the Night of the Carcasses an authentic vision of the future. Of the two conflicting accounts, the four hundred years mentioned in verse 13 and the four generations mentioned in verse 16, the latter is the more likely to be Eisaacic material. (For argument to this effect, see the discussion of the literal fourth generation—Dinah and her brothers—in chapter 5.) In any event, the vision as a whole makes occupation of the land contingent on two Eisaacic concerns—justice and the fullness of time. Yet the overall effect of the speech and the sign that follows it is to conjure the Eisaacic verbal assurance about the subsequent course of history only to eclipse it with the force of the visual drama of present encounter. Therefore, regardless of whether we take the chief precursor text to the Covenant of the Carcasses to be the circumcision covenant in chapter 17 or the speech about prodigy as numerous as stars (15.5), the Covenant of the Carcasses revises an Eisaacic notion of the relation between words and symbols. Whereas the stars in the sky and the rite of circumcision are both "generally understood symbols," Jacob's smoking fire-pot and flaming torch are awe-inspiring wonders. Jacob changes the meaning of "sign."

Beget

While Jacob's revision of the covenant turns normative, "homey" circumcision into an *unheimlich* scenario, Jacob's revision of the annunciation concerning Isaac gloriously heightens the *heimlich* or domestic element to produce an uncanniness of a different sort. The whole scene of the annunciation according to Jacob might be regarded as an exemplary domestication of the sublime—or rather, a story in which such domestication is as much theme as mode. Compare the opening of the visitation scenes in chapters 17 (the Eisaacic account) and 18 (the Jacobic):

> And when Abram was ninety years old and nine, the Lord appeared to Abram and said unto him, "I am the Almighty God. Walk before me, and be thou perfect."
>
> Yava appeared to him by the oaks of Mamre when he was sitting in front of his tent at midday. Abraham looked up and saw three men almost upon him. He no sooner saw than he ran from his tent toward them and bowed low, saying, "My lord, if I have found favor with you, don't pass me by!"

For Eisaac, the injunction "walk before me" expresses, through dead metaphor, a metaphysical stance. Abram's walking "before God" means conducting his life with moral consciousness of the divine Presence. Even the end of the visitation, when the text literally says, "God went up from on Abraham" (17:22), uses a change in physical position to represent an awareness of theological position. But for Jacob, the dead metaphor can come alive again. Jacob's story begins with a sentence that seems to ruminate over a cud too hastily swallowed before: *God appeared to him.* (I attribute to Jacob the substitution of *Yava* for *Elohim* in 17:1, and take as emblem of the "rumination" the reversal *wayyērāʾ YHWH ʾel-ʾabrām* to *wayyērāʾ ʾēlāyw YHWH.* It is as though Jacob paused to ask, "And just how did Yava appear to him?" He answers: "It was like this: You see, there were these three travelers . . ." The sentence introducing the three travelers contains an ordinary idiom, *niṣṣābîm ʿālāyw* (standing over [and against] him), which also, if ruminated slowly, seems to capture the transition from metaphysics to physical stance: As celestial personages, the visitors were *ʿālāyw,* "over" him, and they descend to confront Abraham in the form of earthly travelers.

Two details in what follows help concentrate attention on the transition. First, there is the unusual repetition of *wayyarĕ'* (he looked, he saw): He raised his eyes and saw three men by him; he saw and ran to meet them . . . (18:2). *Wayyarĕ'* becomes a Jacobic tag for a mode of seeing that is more than seeing, "seeing into the life of things"—Eisaacic things. Then there is the peculiar question of how many angels can dance on the pinpointed moment of transition. Abraham sees three, but (except in the Samaritan Hebrew Pentateuch, which normalizes the discrepancy by having Abraham address the three in the plural) he speaks to a second-person-singular one—the One whom he discerns behind the figuration of three: "My lord, if I have found favor in your eyes, do not pass me by." It is as though Abraham, by insisting that the three are one, lingers over the transition from Eisaacic ur-text to Jacobic narrative and mediates between Eisaacic piety and Jacobic play.

Jacob lingers over domestic detail with special reference to the question of who is standing over whom and what sort of slip one can, with grace, "let stand." Abraham's preparations for the meal soon leave him in the position of "standing over" his guests, waiting on them. Although there is nothing but piety and grace in Abraham's posture, we can appreciate his busyness in contrast to—as a contrast to—the singleness of the Eisaacic God's covenantal descent in chapter 17, where it is not till verse 22, when God ascends from Abraham, that we realize he had been "hovering." A little later in the Jacobic narrative, Yava mulls over the wickedness of Sodom and decides, "I'll go down now and have a look." The dignity and singleness of the Eisaacic ascent of God have given way to these comings and goings of divine business. Perhaps the most startling of these ups and downs is the one evidently slighted in the Masoretic text when two of the three celestial creatures continue on to Sodom while Yava himself remains standing before Abraham. This version was apparently too Jacobic for the rabbis, who emended the text to read that Abraham stood before God (18:22). This correction in the service of Eisaacic propriety serves as a fine indicator of just how far in quite a different direction Jacob had moved.

Two possible Jacobic puns accentuate the sweet savor of the revisited annunciation scene. "It has ceased to be with Sarah after the manner of women" (18:11), where *'oraḥ* means "way, manner, length of time" and refers to the menstrual period. In context, however, the word puns on *'ōrēaḥ* (visitor) and reminds us that Abraham's visitors express, in a social sphere, the life, the sexual life, from which Sarah has been excluded. Nobody has been visiting her. Laughing to herself, she questions whether she can still find pleasure when her husband is so old (18:12). The word *'ēden* ("pleasure," as in "Garden of Eden") could suggest *'iddâ,* "menstrual period." Whether we wish to say these puns are present or not intended in the text, they remind us of how different Sarah's inner thought is, in the

Jacobic account, from her husband's reaction in the Eisaacic version. There Abraham laughs at the rather abstract thought that a man of a hundred, a woman of ninety, should have a child. In Jacob's story, Sarah's wonder has less wonder than incredulity: Can the aged Abraham still do it? What follows, in the colloquy between man and God, is "sublime" in a much domesticated or humanized sense. When the incarnate Yava asks *Abraham* why *Sarah* laughed, what he says out loud to Abraham does not exactly repeat Sarah's question of Abraham's capacity; Yava substitutes a rather Eisaacic paraphrase: "Am I really to give birth when I'm old?" What follows is no rigorous exposure of a weakness in faith but something on the order of a tease. Confronted by a supernatural personage with power to see into the heart, Sarah backs off: "Who, me? I didn't laugh!" God makes supremely genial this moment of confrontation by continuing the dispute on all-too-human terms: "Oh, yes you did!" (18:15).

At this point, the domestication of the Eisaacic covenant may appear to be complete. Jacob has brought Sarah into the picture and introduced Yava as a ready third in either of two threesomes. Yava is not only right there, and penetrative of the human heart in a way he was not in Eisaac's story; he colors the entire encounter with a happier, less awesome shade. Though Jacob's story also resembles Eisaac's in deriving Isaac's name from a human laughter, there hovers over the Jacobic account the benignancy of a god who "smiles his work to see." In Eisaac's story, Abraham's laughter to himself is not the subject of an interchange with God, who reacts only to the decorous speech Abraham vocalizes. In clarifying that a son of Sarah, not Ishmael, will be privileged, God returns Abraham to contemplation of the Eisaacic pre-scription or inexorability of His plan: "Thou shalt call his name Isaac, and I will establish my covenant with him for an everlasting covenant, and with his seed after him" (17:19). Jacob does not call the covenant into question, but he reconsiders the burden of the covenant by imagining it as less awesomely arbitrary, more related to the moral fabric of Abraham. It is part of the meaning of the Jacobic annunciation story that it should be tied so closely to the exchange over the fate of Sodom.

We may be surprised—though we should be more delighted than incredulous—to discover that such revision of the annunciation scene in the direction of the domestic, the *heimlich,* comes from the same hand as the eerie or *unheimlich* Covenant of the Carcasses. It is the function of the literary maker (as the English romantics understood) to make the strange more familiar and the familiar more strange. Coleridge describes in *Biographia Literaria* XIV his involvement in persons and characters supernatural, "yet so as to transfer from our inward nature a human interest and a semblance of truth sufficient to procure for these shadows of imagination that willing suspension of disbelief. . . ." He could be speaking about the composition of the Covenant of the Carcasses. But when he goes on to describe the complementary aim of Wordsworth's lyrical ballads, "to excite a feeling analogous to the supernatural by awakening the mind's attention from the lethargy of custom," he could be describing the Jacobic reimagination of the annunciation scene. Jacob pulls Eisaac in both directions, making the supernatural more human, the human "more excited with a feeling analogous to the supernatural"; in Jacob's hands, the canny and uncanny are strangely allied.

Get a Good Deal

The same God who could teasingly uncover Sarah's thought now genially uncovers to Abraham his own intention to have a look and uncover the extent of the wickedness of Sodom. Some scholars have singled out 18:19 (or a larger passage including 18:19) as an interpolation in the J text: "I have known him to the end that he may command his children and his household after him to keep the way of Yava, to do justice and judgment in order that Yava may bring upon Abraham [the handsome reward in posterity] which He has promised him." While this may not sound much like our Jacob, there is no necessity to the assumption that "moral concern" equals "secondary accretion." On the contrary, we can best understand the Jacobic tale of Abraham bargaining with Yava as a midrash or set of midrashim on an "already written" fate of Sodom.

A brief excursus on inside and outside: The question of God dwelling in or among the people recurs in the Bible in stories of rebellion and in contexts where reinterpretation is theme as well as act. In the story of Korah, for example, the rebel cry is that "the whole congregation is holy and Yava within them!" (Num. 16:3). The question of what it means for God to dwell *bĕqereb* or *bĕtôk hāʿām* (in the midst of or "inside" the people) is like the New Testament question (Luke 17:21) of whether the kingdom of God dwells among the people (possibly meaning "in the form of one man in the midst of others") or within the people—within the individual heart. The rebellion at Sinai ostensibly concerns the difficulty in sensing the presence of a god who is both "up there" and "in the midst," and there is some question of whether God can continue to go in the midst of the people (Exod. 33:2–4) or even permit a tabernacle within the camp (Exod. 33:7–11). It is essential priestly doctrine that the tabernacle resides within the people, even *bĕtôk ṭumʾōtām*, "in the midst of their uncleanness" (Lev. 16:16), but the meaning of that "midst" seems to be a persistent point of tension between priest and prophet, observer and reformer, or Eisaacic text and Jacobic voice. When Sarah laughs *bĕqirbāh* (internally, in her womb, "to herself," as we more idiomatically say), Yava shows that he dwells in her midst, hears her inner laugh, and ordains the reformation of that inner word into the flesh of Isaac, the Laugh within the Womb.

The question of Sodom and Gomorrah concerns the fate of the righteous *'ăšer běqirbāh* (who dwell in the city, literally "who are in her womb," 18:24). Yava's question to himself, "Shall I conceal from Abraham what I mean to do?" (18:17) might be considered a question of what is to be left enwombed, what brought to birth in dialogue with Abraham. Let us suppose that the fate of Sodom and Gomorrah was part of the Eisaacic text, a text that contained these elements:

> [Abraham and Lot] separated themselves one from the other. Abraham dwelled in the land of Canaan, and Lot dwelled in the cities of the Plain, moving his tent as far as Sodom. Now the men of Sodom were wicked and sinners against God exceedingly. And God said, "Should I hide from Abraham what I am doing when Abraham will be a great and numerous people, and all the nations of the earth will be blessed in him? I have known him [become intimate with him] because he will [I know] command his children and his household after him to follow God's way and to do justice and righteousness in order that God may bring on Abraham all that he promised him. [God spoke to Abraham, and Abraham interceded for his nephew Lot.] And it came to pass, when God destroyed the cities of the Plain, that God remembered Abraham and sent Lot out of the midst of the overthrow, when he overthrew the cities in which Lot dwelt. (13:11–13, 18:17–19, 19:29)

In this hypothetical reconstruction of an ur-text, I have "restored" the Eisaacic *Elohim* where we now have *Yava,* and I have supposed mention, though a colorless mention, of Abraham's intercession on behalf of Lot. I have also assumed consistency and clarity about the destruction of Sodom and Gomorrah: Abraham prays for Lot, and Lot is spared. The divine will, intent from the beginning on the destruction of the wicked, is not bent.

Whether or not such an ur-text existed, we can safely say that Jacob, and only Jacob, could conceive of Yava going down to take a good look at what is going on in Sodom. My hypothesis is that this divine meditation comes as a reaction against the too determinate fate of the wicked, the "already written" quality of their sin and punishment. Jacob restores the "oral" or present-time nature of contemplation, and in doing so creates a divine model for Abraham. This Abraham is not simply reminding God of a righteous man who must be saved; he is looking to strike a better bargain. Whether the Eisaacic *ṣědāqâ ûmišpāṭ* should be translated "justice and mercy" or "justice and judgment" (18:19), for Jacob there is something too oppressive about an exact system of reward and punishment. Jacob's answer is a Yava who considers the possible difference between what the Sodomites are reported to be doing and what he might himself make of it. In Eisaac's hands, a judge who wants to see for himself might be trying more precisely to make the punishment suit the crime; but for Jacob, the effect is to suggest just the reverse—the possibility of interposing a little ease between the moral outcry and its just retribution.

It is not just the fate of the Sodomites but the Eisaacic text of 19:29 (the unadorned announcement that "God destroyed the cities of the Plain") that Jacob defers. He defers it with two tales of deferral: First, Abraham detains Yava Himself. Having announced—and announced, we might believe, to Abraham as well as the general readership—that he is on his way to Sodom, Yava is arrested by Abraham and his haggling over numbers. Although we use the expression "cheapening" to describe ordinary market bargaining, Abraham is by no means cheapening justice; he may be literally attempting to cheapen the price of redemption (ten for one are the final terms), but so coarse a phrase must not obscure the high morality of a generous salvation. Whether or not there is any historical truth to the ur-text I have hypothesized, there remains the moral truth of the difference between an Eisaacic fate (Lot was worthy, Lot was saved, 19:29) and a Jacobic ambition to save the many on the merit of the few.

The second, no less beautiful tale of deferral is that of Lot and his visitors. The story may have been based on (rather than a base for) the hideous tale of the men of Gibeah, Judges 19–20. The story may also have had an origin in a verbal rather than a moral outrage—the pun on *deʿâ* as judgmental or carnal knowledge. Eisaac's God "knows" Abraham in 18:19; Jacob's Sodomites would "know" Yava's representatives (19:5). Whatever its private inspiration or folk origin, this story multiplies the modes and complicates the morality of delay. Lot's virtue is first manifest in his hospitality, expressed as the desire to detain the strangers overnight. In contrast, the viciousness of the Sodomites is expressed as sexual impatience: They want to know those strangers right now, the first night, before they go to sleep. Lot stalls for time, talking to them while closing the door behind him—as though he could thus give his guests a few minutes' more peace even if he lost the larger struggle over them. Even the supernatural intervention of Lot's guests takes on the character of a special form of delay: The Sodomites are stricken with blindness so that they cannot find the house door—or cannot find it easily. Suddenly the valence of delay shifts, and the visitors are all haste in collecting Lot and his family. Now it is first Lot and then his wife who delay, the second permanently. We are hastening not simply before the coming of the fire and the brimstone but before the closure that must come all too soon with the return to the prescribed ending of the Eisaacic story: God remembers Abraham, saves Lot, and destroys the cities of the Plain.

Although the Jacobic Lot story ends with a peculiar piece of jingoistic nastiness that may well have been dictated by extraliterary motives, we can also place the story of Lot's incest with his daughters in the context of tales about haste. Now that Sodom and Gomorrah have been destroyed, there seems to be leisure for a fiction with no morality at all. But it is only the appearance of amorality, sanctioned by the special dispensation for non-Israelite genealogies. Actually, the moral question of haste vs. patience is very much there. As we hear Lot's eldest daughter reasoning that they'll *never* find a man (i.e., that no marriageable male is available right now), we are struck by the contrast to the story of Abraham and Sarah's patience. We turn back to Eisaac—we turn to the story of Isaac—with renewed confidence in the value of biding one's narrative or existential time.

·4·

THE DISAPPEARANCES OF ISAAC

> The angels bore him to Paradise, where he tarried three years, to be healed from the wound inflicted upon him by Abraham on the occasion of the *akedah.*
>
> —*Yalkut Reubeni,* cited by Shalom Spiegel in *The Last Trial*

The Banishment of Ishmael

According to the traditional documentary hypothesis, the birth of Isaac in chapter 21 is an event so momentous that J, E, and P all recorded it; more important, the redactor felt some urgency about preserving at least a snippet of each account, as though these three source-strata were magi, some note of whose gift of acknowledgment to the sacred babe had to be on the record. The (slightly reconstructed) acknowledgments might look like this:

> **J:** Yava visited Sarah as he had said. Sarah conceived and bore Abraham a son in his old age.
> **E:** [God] did to Sarah what he had spoken. Sarah said, "God has made a jest of me! Everyone who sees me will laugh at me."
> **P:** [God remembered Abraham, and God fulfilled his promise to Abraham] at the set time of which God had spoken to him. Abraham called the name of his son—the son whom Sarah bore him—Isaac.

In the interest of harmonization, the *Elohim* of E (though not of P in verse 2) became *Yava,* and some introductory formula of the P account dropped out.

Although it may not be possible to refute such a hypothesis, it is possible to imagine an alternate one a little better at accounting for some of the details. If we suppose an Eisaacic account especially concerned to narrate the birth of its hero with due solemnity and attention, then the repetitive element noted by the documentarians belongs, rather, to the formality of prose heightened to the status of verse:

> Elohim visited Sarah as he had said; Elohim did to Sarah as he had spoken. Sarah conceived, and bore Abraham a son in his old age; at the set time of which Elohim had spoken to him.
>
> Abraham called the name of his son, whom Sarah bore to him, Isaac; Abraham circumcised his son Isaac when he was eight days old, as Elohim had commanded him. Sarah said, "Elohim has made a jest of me; everyone who hears will laugh at me." And she said: "Who is it who would have pronounced about Abraham, 'Sarah gives suck to men-children'? I have born him a son in his old age."

We may suppose that this set piece remained entirely intact in the transmission from Eisaacic to Jacobic hands—except that Jacob substitutes *Yava* for *Elohim* when introducing the glorious doings. As Jacob transmits the text, it is Yava who "does things," perhaps even with a hint of more than overseeing them in that strange "did to Sarah" of verse 1b. From Jacob's perspective, there would be something appropriate in leaving *Elohim* as the agent who did the talking originally; Jacob leaves *Elohim* in verse 2b, and of course in 4c. But the major decision Jacob makes is to leave intact the story of Hagar and Ishmael that he found in this context, and to write his own Hagar story that "prevents" this one—in the root, Miltonic sense of going before and coming up with an original piece:

> See how from far upon the eastern road
> The star-led wizards haste with odors sweet!
> O run, prevent them with thy humble ode,
> And lay it lowly at his blessed feet;
> Have thou the honor first thy Lord to greet,
>   And join thy voice unto the angel choir,
> From out his secret altar touched with hallowed fire.
> ("Nativity Ode")

We need to examine first the magic of the Eisaacic story of the weaning of Isaac and the banishment of Ishmael. We can then try to imagine how a precursor-wizard, with odors sweet, might be met with a pinch of fishier fume.

Were there numerous events narrated in the life of young Isaac, we might believe that one verse tells us about an infant, while a later one shows us Sarah catching Ishmael making homosexual overtures to a half-brother sometime near puberty (21:9). But since the description of Ishmael "playing" follows immediately on the celebration of Isaac's weaning, I think we must associate the sight of the boys at play with a much earlier stage. Sarah simply sees Ishmael *mĕṣaḥēq* (playing, laughing, "Isaacing")—a sight perhaps even more innocent in the Masoretic text, which lacks the normalizing predicate "with Isaac." There is no consideration of the relationship between the mothers, no sense of a representative trial of

Ishmael's character, followed by a punishment that suits the crime. There is no crime—except in the colloquial sense of "shame" or sadness at an unfortunate but inevitable event. Instead of psychological insight into all-too-human jealousies, Eisaac's account is so brief that its very abstraction from emotional entanglement seems a pious interpretation of Sarah's motives as spiritual service.

We are given only the barest mention of Abraham's distress before this too is cut short in deference to the divine plan. God intervenes to exact Abraham's obedience and to reassure Abraham—with no extra words, for in matters related to divine choice Eisaac writes with the brevity of authority rather than the lingerings of emotional ambivalence—that all shall ultimately be well for Ishmael too. Then a sentence of surprising detail, wonderful in its own right and all the more special for its relationship to the *ʿăqēdâ* story that follows: "And Abraham rose up early in the morning, and took bread, and a bottle of water, and gave them to Hagar, putting [those things] on her shoulder—and the child—and sent her away." What to do with that child clearly posed some problem in the redaction of the text: The Septuagint has the child on Hagar's shoulder, while the Masoretic text seems to have the jug of water on the shoulder, the child handed over to her without a verb for the action, as though it were too fraught with pathos for any verb. In accounting for the uncertainty about whether the child is on her shoulder or walking by her side, the standard documentary hypothesis provides a plausible explanation: the Hagar-Ishmael tale of chapter 21 is an old E tale, with Ishmael a young child; the Hagar story of chapter 16 is an old J tale. P, reconciling the two into chronological sequence, adds the specification that Abraham was eighty-six when Ishmael was born (16:15). This makes Ishmael fourteen at the birth of Isaac, fifteen-plus when sent away. And so P, or a redactor who knows P, deletes the phrase (preserved or restored in the Septuagint) that put Hagar's child on her shoulder.

Yet I wonder if there is any temporal priority to the carriable-child text. Those who argue for its antiquity point to the divine directive of 21:18: *qûmî, śĕʾî ʾet-hannaʿar,* which they translate, "arise, lift up the child," as though the child formerly carried is being carried anew. Yet the very same verse continues, *wĕhaḥăzîqî ʾet-yādēk bô* (hold him with your hand). It seems more probable that the child was originally led by the hand, that he is relinquished to his death throes under a bramble, and that he is lifted in the sense of being helped from his near-terminal weakness and prone position, and once more led by the hand when the angel so directs Hagar. As an exquisitely wrought Eisaacic text with strong ties to the *ʿăqēdâ* story, this story of Hagar and Ishmael privileges the image of Hagar and son going off, hand in hand. The verbs for lifting and casting down accentuate the pathos and the parallelism: Hagar casts the child (or sends him away) under a bramble; the verb *wattašlēk* may be evoked when the angel tells Abraham *'al tišlaḥ* (do not *cast forth* your hand against the child). Hagar lifts the child (*śĕ'î 'et-hanna'ar*) as she and Abraham lift their eyes: such lifting is the uplifting gesture of faith. Perhaps this is the special poignancy of Hagar lifting her voice in lamentation—something she does in the Masoretic, though not in the Septuagint, text. Lifting her voice in lamentation is another idiom, an all-too-human idiom, and the angel ignores that kind of "lifting." He reports that God is responding to the cry *of the child.*

Compassion is terribly important for Eisaac, almost as important as—and wherever possible, concomitantly set forth with—the inexorability of the divine plan. Here, the loss to Abraham of his firstborn is restituted by the opportunity the story opens up for divine compassion and even tenderness. An angel of God calls out, "What is the matter, Hagar?"—or perhaps the intimacy of *mâ-lāk* might be better represented by King James: "What aileth thee, Hagar?" The question marks no indifference to or ignorance of her fate but rather the gentlest of conversational openers—something like Hamlet's "How is it with you, lady?" when urged by the ghost of his father to comfort Gertrude. Neither Hagar nor Ishmael is said to have prayed for assistance, and the divine response is neither to the faith such prayer would imply nor to the merits of their case. The angel announces God's responsiveness to the cry of pure distress, the cry of the lad himself: "Have no fear; God has heard the voice of the lad where he is." To appreciate the purity of this utterance, we can contrast the moral point of a later midrash. Rashi interprets "where he is" as a question of moral stance. Ministering angels, in support of the "prosecuting attorney," bring testimony against Ishmael from the actions of his descendants. The supreme judge throws out the evidence and asks simply, "What is he now, righteous or evil?" When they reply "righteous," God announces that the scales of judgment tip toward Ishmael, in favor of his present redemption, because of his present innocence. All this is precisely what is *not* in the Eisaacic tale. God has heard the voice of the lad where he is physically—in distress—and not where he is on a scale of moral virtue. God sees and God opens Hagar's eyes so she can see his beneficent presence—in the form of the much-needed well. The purity of such a tale might be called "pastoral" in the sophisticated, literary sense of a recasting of complex problems into a magically simple setting; the story is also "pastoral" in the sense that the god who watches over people regardless of their wanderings is the protector-god of shepherds and other wanderers who may have to cross deserts and abandon previously established sites of worship. As anthropologists have discovered in surveying African religions, for example, there is no reason to regard the concept of a genius loci as more primitive than monotheistic belief in a deity of transnational provenience; deities limited to one locale may be the product not of more primitive but of more partisan, belated, civic interest. Eisaac's Hagar story reveals the workings of a god yet unsullied by the partisan interests of those who keep a certain shrine.

In the intertextual equivalent of family romance, as well as in the theology of Eisaac itself, we can discern a paternal benignity that can more easily be differed from than "improved upon." Jacob's struggle for place may yield some extraordinary versions of Eisaacic stories, but in terms of both literary genre and theology, there is nothing inherently more civilized about the Jacobic point of view. Those masterly old stories that tell of a compassionate God watchful of his creatures' needs are stories particularly difficult to "improve." The Eisaacic Hagar story, perhaps just because it concerns displacement from Abraham's home and line of inheritance, takes pains to outline a world in which all may be perceived as *heimlich*—a world in which all peoples, alone or together, can feel "at home." It is left for Jacob to puncture the rainbow-colored bubble of universalistic glow and to do something that may be of questionable moral improvement but that finds vitality in the difference.

What does Jacob, master of the uncanny, make of such a mellowed tale? In terms of narrative sequence, Jacob's Hagar story does not follow upon Eisaac's; it precedes and preempts, or almost preempts, the beautiful story told by Eisaac. Eisaac's story centers on the weaning of Isaac and the (somewhat analogous) painful separation of the chosen from the unchosen line. Jacob's story reverts to an earlier point, the time when Ishmael is conceived but not yet biologically separated from his mother. It may be that Jacob's Hagar story represents a midrashic expansion on a previously coherent, though less interesting, text made up of 16:4a and 16:15. The sequence *wattahar, wattēled* (she conceived, and she bore [a son to Abraham], 21:2) suggests that there may have been a similar sequence represented by *wattahar* in 16:4a and *wattēled* of 16:15, a sequence broken by Jacob to insert his strange version of the Hagar story.

Jacob finds only the briefest mention of Sarai's plan in Eisaac's narrative: "Sarai, the wife of Abram, bore him no children; she had an Egyptian maid named Hagar. Sarai, Abram's wife, took Hagar her Egyptian maid, after Abram had dwelt in Canaan ten years, and gave her to Abram her husband for a wife" (16:1a, 3). Into this, Jacob inserts a bit of thinking out loud: Sarai assigns the cause of her barrenness, not the cure, to Yava; she proposes to Abram that they take matters into their own hands by coupling Abram and Sarai's maid. The strange pun on *'ibbāneh* ("I will be built up through her" or "I will get sons by her")—a pun repeated two generations later when Rachel and Leah compete with each other for Jacob's seed—suggests that the matriarch's desire is less for the proper construing of God's intent to multiply descendants than it is for the construction of a monument to herself. Shades of the tower of Babel. And her babble—her idea of confusing not mother tongues but mothers—wins Abram's ear. In Eisaac's Hagar story, Eisaac's God intervenes to reassure Abram that the voice of Sarai is the voice of God; but there is no like assurance here—at least not yet. First, Jacob's narrative shifts from black and white to color, and the true colors Sarai and Hagar show are not the most attractive. Hagar turns pride to disrespect, while Sarai turns jealousy of Hagar into hostility toward Abram. And Abram, who in Eisaac's story at least gets a chance to be described as disapproving of the treatment of Hagar, here becomes a cipher. There is no divine sanction of Sarai's treatment of Hagar, only the poor patriarch's desire to avoid a fight. What he tells her literally is, "Do whatever is good in your eyes" (16:6)—which means, or which she takes to mean, "Be as mean as you like—just leave me alone."

Though the supernatural makes a more delayed appearance in this tale, its uncanniness is notably increased. Read by itself, this is is a story in which Hagar moves away from Abram without divine intercession. Read as a revision of the Eisaacic Hagar story, this account has Hagar proceed even further—past her hour of sorest need to the discovery of water—before the appearance of an angel of Yava by the fountainside. The scene could have been set by Kafka or by Thomas Mann: What the angel says is, "Well now, Hagar, Sarai's maid, just where do you come from and where do you think you're going?" But his presence at the fountain before Hagar arrives speaks a different message: "'What took you so long? I have been waiting for you!"

Hagar responds to the uncanny authority of the stranger by answering the first of his actual questions promptly and straightforwardly and remaining silent on the second. Where is she going indeed? Eisaac's Hagar episode, situated later in the Abraham story, can focus also on latter-day sociological facts: the children of Ishmael are half-brothers, outside the covenant and hostile to the children of Isaac. But Jacob's Hagar story can at most serve as a covert reflection of the situation of Jacob himself: He can step tangentially into the narrative wilderness, but he must circle back. The directive to Hagar, "Return to your mistress and humble yourself under her hands," is a directive that spells also the limit of midrashic originality. Hagar is free to wander but is bound to return.

Further interpretation of Jacob's Hagar story is restricted by our ignorance about whether, or how severely, the story as we have it has been cut. Verses 9, 10, and 11 may have been three parts of a dialogue the intervening responses of which have been lost:

> 9. Yava's angel said to her: Return to your mistress and humble yourself under her hands.

> 10. Yava's angel said to her: I will greatly multiply your progeny; they will be too numerous to count.
> 11. Yava's angel said to her: Behold! You are pregnant and will give birth to a son. Call his name *yišmāʿēʾl* [God hears] because Yava has heard your affliction [same root as "humble yourself"].

Yet whether or not there were intervening objections from Hagar, the major discontinuity is not between these three verses but between the unit of these three and the rather disconcerting revelation that follows:

> 12. He will be a wild ass of a man, with his hands into everything and everyone's hand against him; he will dwell in the presence of all his brothers.

Whatever the precise meaning of that last phrase, it is nothing too savory, nothing to comfort a mother-to-be in a hostile household. With Yeats, Hagar might well wonder what mother

> Would think her son, did she but see that shape
> With sixty or more winters on its head
> A compensation for the pang of his birth,
> Or the uncertainty of his setting forth?

But even uncertainty would be a greater comfort. To know that your son will be a wild ass of a man, a father of outlaws or homeless wretches, is to be punished far more than any mere promise of numbers can compensate.

At this point, two very different paths are open to the interpreter. One is to acknowledge that we tend to underread Eisaac and to give Jacob the benefit of the doubt, when it is more probable that the pathos we would wish Jacob to extend belongs exclusively to Eisaac. In this view, the revelation of Yava to Hagar in verse 12 is raw Jacob, and a reminder of the moral crudity and nationalistic priorities of this partisan writer. The other possibility is to trust that we know Jacob well enough by now to recognize that *verse 12 is not his voice.* The fact that *pereʾ* (wild ass) is not otherwise Pentateuchal may serve as a clue; another is that a second redactional context (25:18) contains the peculiar idiom about Ishmael living in the presence of brothers. But the chief reason I propose (and prefer) this reading is that without verse 12 the text coheres in a characteristically Jacobic manner:

> 11. Behold, you are pregnant; you will bear a child and call him Ishmael because Yava has heard your affliction.
> 13. She called Yava, who spoke to her, *ʾēl rŏʾî* ("God has seen me" or possibly "A God visible to me") "because," she said, *hăgam hălōm rāʾîtî ʾaḥărê rŏʾî* ("here I have been able to see after being seen," or "here I have looked after him who saw me").

Verse 13 may take on special meaning if we see it as a reaction to the play on *tîr'î/wattēre'* (fear not/she saw) in the climax of the Eisaacic Hagar story, 21:17–19. In addition, the strange *'aḥărê* (after) remains a characteristic of some specially heightened and problematic passages—in the *'ăqēdâ* and in Exodus 33. What is peculiarly Jacobic here is not simply Hagar's rich play on words but the relationship of this interest in sight to the interest in hearing that the angel has just proclaimed. He says, "God hears your affliction," and she says, "I triumph in my sight." This kind of turn—this attention to figurative language and the substitution of one sensory trope for another—reflects a particularly heightened *literary* sense. We are approaching what may be regarded as the core scene of interaction between Eisaac and Jacob, a scene whose interpretation will hinge upon reconsideration of what has been heard, what might be seen.

The Undoing of the *'ăqēdâ*

My readers will not be surprised that I find the meaning of the extraordinary *'ăqēdâ* narrative (chapter 22) to be all involved with the struggle between Eisaac and Jacob. But it is worth pausing to note that scholars of the documentary hypothesis have also had to struggle with the attribution of the episode and what this means from the perspective of the entire scheme. The problem can be represented by a few admirably honest sentences in Speiser's *Genesis:* "The narrative is attributed to E with scarcely a dissenting voice, and with only a few minor reservations. . . . On internal evidence, however, based on style and content, the personality behind the story should be J's. . . . The issue is thus not a closed one by any means."

Does the story have *a* personality? Anyone who wishes to attribute the entire story to J must ignore the discrepancy between "God put Abraham to the test" and virtually everything we elsewhere discover about the relations between Yava and his heroes. Anyone wishing to attribute the entire story to E must ignore the muddle of endings "in the school of J." Even granted the option of attributing to E the story minus the intervention of the angel of Yava as we have it, one must be struck with the highly wrought verbal texture and psychological complexity of the interaction between Abraham and Isaac. The story at its height seems to be "essence of E" with a purity nowhere else found.

A hypothesis of a mixed origin ought to help in the appreciation of this story—the story as we have it, or at least some "purer form" glimpsed behind the form in which it has come to us. Those who hold to the anteriority of J could present a case for the normalization of an uncanny story by the imposition, on a J narrative, of an Elohist "cover fiction" that the whole thing is a test of Abraham's faith. What would the J text have looked like without the framing device as we have it? Perhaps such an ur-version threw us in medias res, like Exod. 4:24, into a confrontation with the utterly uncanny: "Yava sought to slay Isaac"—or even "Yava sought to slay Abraham . . . and Abraham took his son. . . ." Such a hypothesis may help explain what we have, at least in the beginning of the tale, as an attempt by a later and more "religious" consciousness to raise the arbitrary into the realm of the sophisticated providential; but we do not receive much help from such a hypothesis in understanding the Elohist nature of the center of the story or its problematic end.

Let us return to the idea of Jacob the revisionist and consider the "trial of faith" as the *given.* It is hard to use the English word "faith" without evoking a religious value as alien to Jacob as is Christianity itself. Jacob does not have "faith." He does know the fear of Yava, the fear of a powerful force who just might, if pressed, prove arbitrary. And he also knows an emotion that is legitimately represented by the Hebrew *ʾĕmûnâ,* but not to be translated "faith." It is trust, trust in Yava's reasonability exceeding his wrath, trust in his benevolence beyond his uncanniness. But the God who puts Abraham to the test is calling for a "faith" not very Hebrew (as Jacob conceives Hebrew), one more like that of the book of Hebrews: "the substance of things hoped for, the evidence of things not seen" (11:1). To represent how foreign, how repulsive to Jacob is the theology represented by the opening sentence of the *ʿăqēdâ* story, we might consider what the book of Hebrews takes to be Abraham's faith: "He that had received the promises offered up his only begotten son . . . accounting that God was able to raise him up, even from the dead" (11:17–19). I do not believe that Jacob, or any other Hebrew of his time, could have conceived of a literal resurrection from the dead—even if Jacob had set out to write the *ʿăqēdâ* story as a parody of what he took to be Eisaacic spirituality; but I think it almost as preposterous that Jacob should have conceived of a Yava who would toy with his creatures, teasing Abraham with the possibility of cutting off all hope of the fulfillment of the promise through Isaac.

Were Jacob parodying the Eisaacic mode, we could say that the *ʿăqēdâ* story begins with a swerve against, a demonic exaggeration of, a "faith" we heard about in the Eisaacic Hagar story: "Whatever Sarah says—heed her voice, for your line will be perpetuated through Isaac" (21:12). The *ʿăqēdâ* would begin thus with a swerve against the orthodoxy of listening to Sarah's voice. Now it would be God's own voice (the voice of Elohim, Eisaac's God) that announces a similarly unwelcome thought—a thought similar in that it cuts Abraham off from his child, but a thought more radical in that death rather than expulsion is the form of devastation announced. Abraham's dutiful obedience in the *ʿăqēdâ* story ("He rose early in the morning . . .") and the pathos in the conversation of father and son (22:7–8) would appear to be parodic repetitions of similar elements in the Eisaacic Hagar story.

I *do* wish to argue that the *ʿăqēdâ* story has a special relation to the Eisaacic Hagar story—but it is not a relation of belated parodist to an earlier literary form. Imitations and rewritings are to be found, in Genesis and throughout the Bible, but parody as such is at once too daring and too simple a mode of relation of one biblical story to another in the same circle of events. Let us first specify the relation of the *ʿăqēdâ* story to its predecessor within the Eisaacic corpus, and then consider what Jacob might have found to do.

When we read that Abraham rose early to set Hagar on her way (21:14), we can fill in several motives for this attentiveness to the divine injunction. Either Abraham is solicitous about Hagar and eager to see her settled somewhere before sundown, or he is eager to get the whole nasty business off his hands, or he hastens to obey a divine command. In turning to the Isaac story, we seem to be viewing a purified zeal, for since there is no question of kindly regard for the future of *this* outcast, pious attentiveness seems to be the reason for Abraham's haste. This religiosity culminates in the picture of Abraham, after three days, lifting up his eyes to descry the place in the distance. Such a gesture, or more accurately such an attitude, is that of Religious Man, lacking the substance of things hoped for, searching for evidence of things not seen. Hagar "lifted up" not her eyes but her voice, for Hagar is not Religious Woman personified but a natural woman in distress. The pathos of that outcry is emphasized by the isolation of Hagar from her son (from whom she distanced herself so as not to look upon his death) and by the heavenly response that is specifically not to the cry of Hagar but to the unmentioned, almost unmentionable cry of the child.

On the third day (an Eisaacic tag—cf. 31:22; 40:13, 19; 42:17) Abraham sees the place from a distance. In portraying Abraham raising his eyes in the attitude of Religious Man, Eisaac "refines" the Hagar story by intensifying the purity of religious attitude without diminishing the pathetic. Hagar sitting separate from Ishmael, Hagar saying, "I shall not see the death of the child" (21:16) exemplifies Imagination Penetrative—the nobility of the poet's calling in exhibiting the human heart's sorrows. But the comfort Hagar receives in that story seems only incidentally related to her sorrow. An angel of Elohim says *ʾal tîrʾî* ("have no fear!" with the verbs for sight and fear looking alike) and Hagar does "see"—she sees not death but a well of water (21:19). All this seems so much verbal accident until we get to the *ʿăqēdâ* story. Now Isaac sees, as Hagar saw, what is literally before him: "Here is the fire and the butcher's knife, but where is the sacrificial lamb?" Abraham's answer this time carries as much pathos *and* religious spirit as language can bear: "God will provide the lamb for sacrifice, my son!"

The Hebrew is *yirʾeh-lô,* which does, idiomatically, mean "provide." We have, in support of this contention, the evidence of Gen. 41:33, where

Joseph tells Pharaoh to "provide a discreet and wise man to administer Egypt." "Keep your eye out for a really shrewd fellow," Joseph says, but what this Eisaacic text tells us is that God keeps an eye out; God will provide. In the *ʿăqēdâ* story one can argue whether Abraham or Isaac will be "shown" the sacrificial lamb; perhaps *yirʾeh-lô* might best be translated that God will provide for himself a sacrificial lamb. Whatever the translation, the force of the passage comes from the rich irony that this most human, most moving of conversations is also Abraham's most Eisaacic moment of faith: Abraham's speech is in tune with divine providence; his assertion, or his gentle evasion that "God will provide" proves to be a perfect estimation of the providential design.

In the conversation between Abraham and Isaac, the reader faces a peculiar temptation. So moving is this scene, so extraordinary is Abraham's response, that one is tempted to cry "interpolation!" and to fix the repeated phrase, "the two of them walked on together" (22:6, 8) as the mark of the seam. (There is a similar temptation in regard to the repeated phrase about Hagar, that she "sat apart," 21:16a, 16c.) It is a temptation to be resisted, for this conversation marks no Jacobic correction but a pure Eisaacic moment, a moment of pathos and of faith, a moment of unusual coincidence of the Contemplative and the Penetrative. *Were* this an interpolation, we might say that Isaac asks a question Jacobic in its literalism, while Abraham gives a response Eisaacic in its piety. But there is no philological evidence of a separate source for the conversation, and it is hard to imagine an *ʿăqēdâ* story without it. Indeed, the pathos and dramatic irony that the conversation introduce are at the center of the Eisaacic meaning. Here, if anywhere, is the triumph of Eisaac—and perhaps the greatest challenge to Jacobic ingenuity.

It is not unreasonable to suppose that the *ʿăqēdâ* story ended, like the Eisaacic Hagar story, with an angel of Elohim arresting Abraham at the climactic moment:

> An angel of Elohim called to him from heaven and said, "Abraham, Abraham!" He said, "Here I am." He said, "Cast not your hand forth against the child. Don't do anything to him! For now I know that you fear Elohim, since you did not withhold your son, your only son, from me."
>
> Abraham raised his eyes, and looked, and—behold! a ram caught in the thicket by his horns! Abraham went and took the ram and offered him up as a burnt offering instead of his son.
>
> Abraham returned to his servants, and they rose up and went together to Beer-sheba. Abraham dwelt at Beer-sheba.

In *Genesis 1–11: A Commentary,* Claus Westermann argues that the phrase *wayyarĕʾ wĕhinnēh* (he looked and—behold) "is typical of J's narrative style" (p. 449). It may well be that verse 22:13 as we have it already reflects the tinkering of Jacob. If so, it is conceivable that the famous crux about that ram who is *'aḥar* ("behind him," in place of *'eḥad,* "one") also represents no scribal accident but the revisionary hand by which the lamb turns from divine forethought to an emblem of revisionary labor itself: the lamb is *'aḥēr,* "other," and *'aḥar,* "afterthought, other thought," mascot, as it were, of the revisionist as redeemer. With or without such intervention in verse 13, Jacob would be responsible for altering the name of the savior deity. It is Elohim, Eisaac's god, who tested Abraham's faith. But it is Yava, in the text as it is transmitted to us, whose angel proclaims the redemption of Isaac.

Although the story, with the last-minute redemption of Isaac, is an Eisaacic story, perhaps *the* Eisaacic story, Jacob bequeaths it to us as a story about the redemptiveness of the Jacobic perspective. Changing the angel to an angel of Yava, Jacob proclaims that the voice that arrests Abraham's hand is *the voice of Jacob.*

One may regard this twist as the saddest of revisions, representing a failure of imagination in the face of a supreme achievement of a wholly different order. Were the change from *mal'ak 'ĕlōhîm* to *mal'ak YHWH* the extent of Jacobic revision to the *'ăqēdâ* story, we could say that part of the "meaning" of the composite tale is the humbling of an all-too-human effort before one which is "wholly other." That is, the failure of Jacob in the face of Eisaac's brilliant achievement would be like the recognition of human limits before God. Even if we grant that verses 22:14–18 are of the Jacobic revision, such a weak coda seems to come as little more than applause to an achievement that is different in mode, different in outlook.

There is, however, one other possibility suggested by the meaning of the substitution of an angel of Yava for an angel of Elohim. If we take seriously the idea that this change represents no weak-minded harmonist's tinkering but the strong will of Jacob the revisionist, then we should also take seriously the idea that the voice of Jacob is dramatically, self-referentially represented in the act of intervention into an Eisaacic story. In this reading, verses 15–18 represent no careless harmonization of an E and J version of the same tale but a most careful, though covert, undermining of the Eisaacic tale itself. Abraham is blessed, Yava announces, "because you heeded my voice" (22:18). And what is the voice of Yava? The revision of God's will in verses 11–12. Or let us specify two revisions: First, verses 11–12 as they were to be found in Eisaac's story represented a revision of the divine will that was expressed in 22:1–2. And second, verses 11–12, with Jacob's "correction" of *Elohim* to *Yava,* represent the revisionist's notion of what is "really" God's will. Jacob thus has an irony all his own, an irony with which to overgo the Eisaacic irony about Elohim "providing." Jacob's irony is that *in rewarding Abraham for hearkening to his voice, Yava means not the voice of Elohim that in verse 2 commanded the sacrifice of Isaac, but the voice of Yava that in verse 12 forbids it.* The blessing accrues to Abraham "because you heeded *my* voice," the voice of Yava in verse 12 prohibiting the sacrifice of Isaac.

Such a reading hinges on the interpretation of an insufficiently definite pronoun in verse 16. "By myself I have sworn," announces Yava in a fit of Yava-selfhood, Yava-distinctness, "that because you did this thing . . ." What thing? For Eisaac "this thing" so commendable is obviously Abraham's willingness to sacrifice Isaac. But is "this thing" the same thing for Jacob? Might not *this* thing, for Jacob, be Abraham's willingness to heed the voice of Yava, the voice forbidding the sacrifice? We ought then to read *ḥāśaktā* this time to mean not "withheld" (withheld Isaac from me) but "restrained" (kept in bondage, kept to the hideous, Shylockean "bond"). Because you listened to my voice, the true voice of Yava, Abraham, and did not keep Isaac in bonds on the altar, therefore you shall indeed be blessed. And behold a wonder: Originally, in the Eisaacic text, Elohim releases Abraham because Abraham had not withheld Isaac from Elohim. But in Jacob's addition, at least in the Masoretic text, Abraham is praised for not restraining Isaac. Missing from this verse, though supplied by some would-be "correctors," is the word *mimmennî,* "from me." Precisely so: Elohim let Abraham off the hook for not withholding Isaac *from him,* but Yava blessed Abraham for not further restraining Isaac. Later midrashim will elaborate the impulse of an all-too-Eisaacic Abraham to do something to Isaac: "Can I not have permission even to wound him a little?" Abraham will ask; and Yava will reply, *ʿal-taʿaś lō mĕʾûmmâ* ("Don't you dare give him so much as a scratch!"). But the seed for such midrash may have been already planted by the essentially midrashic nature of Jacob's response to the Eisaacic text. Jacob's Abraham is rewarded for heeding the voice of Yava, and the voice of Yava is the voice of the supreme midrashist, Jacob.

The Dissociation of Lot

Were the possibility disproven that Jacob has tampered with the ending of the *ʿăqēdâ* story, the historical fact would remain that for over twenty-five hundred years, readers have been tampering with the story as we have it and supplying conversations between Abraham and God or excuses for the lack of conversation between Abraham and God—conversations that would make a little more Jacobic a text so eerily "other." One of the most persistent forms that the desire for such conversation takes is the question "Why does Abraham not bargain with God over Isaac as he bargained with God over Sodom and Gomorrah?" We may represent as Jacobic the sentiment behind such a question if we isolate the Jacobic protest "Why does Abraham not bargain with God over Isaac?"—and then supply the Jacobic answer "Let him bargain with God over Sodom and Gomorrah!" I am hardly the first to propose that the conversation of Abraham with God over the destruction of Sodom and Gomorrah is midrash that has been incorporated into an earlier, sparser account; but the norm among documentarians is to regard as original, J material Yahweh's decision to examine Sodom at first hand, and to see as late midrash the concern over justice, the decision to tell Abraham what is to come, and Abraham's protest.

Two verbal details suggest that the whole Sodom adventure may be a Jacobic reaction against the Eisaacic story of the *ʿăqēdâ*. The solemn examination of Abraham's faith begins with the phrase *hāʾĕlōhîm nissāh ʾet-ʾabrāhām* (God tested Abraham). If one broods over that verb (*nsh*) with a questioning spirit, one might conceive of its homonym *nśʾ*, whose meaning is "to bear, to take away." In the Sodom story, Abraham asks, *haʾap tispeh wĕlōʾ-tiśśāʾ lammāqôm?*—Will you destroy and not carry away [the iniquity of] the place? (18:24). This sentence has its own verbal play, for both *tispeh* and *tiśśāʾ* can mean "carry away." In context, *tispeh* means "snatch away from the face of the earth"—destroying the whole city because of the wicked inhabitants in it. Abraham questions whether the righteous shall be snatched away with the wicked, whether God will not rather "bear away" the iniquity of the city as a whole, thus freeing the place from the burden of guilt of some of its inhabitants. The question constitutes not just a humble plea for mercy but a little trial of Yava's justice: Which kind of "carrying away" is truest to your nature, Yava? Are you a god who tests people's faith, or is it your nature to grant the benefit of doubt? But the real force of Abraham's question in 18:24 may best be felt if one sees in it a reaction to the Eisaacic trial of Abraham's faith. Eisaac pictures Elohim putting Abraham on trial. Jacob reacts by picturing Abraham putting Yava on trial. It is curious that the most blatant support for this view has routinely been construed as a textual error: We read "Yava stood before Abraham" (19:22) as though Yava stood on trial in the conversation that follows; but the text is conventionally emended, "Abraham stood before Yava," which it certainly would have read were Eisaac, not Jacob, its author.

Eisaac's trial of Abraham ends when God knows that Abraham is *yĕrēʾ ʾĕlōhîm*, a "God-fearing" man (22:12). But just as the Jacobic Hagar story has Yava "already there," waiting by the well rather than appearing out of heaven when it is almost too late, so Jacob has God's knowledge of Abraham precede the revisionary trial. We can regard the Eisaacic conclusion, *kî ʿattâ yādaʿtî*—for now I know (that you are God-fearing) (22:12)—as the

Jacobic point of origin: *kî yĕdaʿtîw*—I know him, or "I have made myself known to him" (18:19). Yava's prevenient knowledge may be read as a trope for the prevenience Jacob gives his story over that already encoded as Eisaac's. Perhaps a similar remark can be made about the scurrilous business in Sodom itself: The Sodomites attack Lot for setting himself up as judge of others—he who was just a visitor, a stranger, now lords it over them in moral judgment (19:9)! Abraham's question of the justice of the Judge of all the earth is thus parodied in the tale itself. Even the desire of the Sodomites to "know" those visitors can be read as a perversion of God's desire to visit the Sodomites the better to know what is going on there; the moral outrage he encounters represents (and in a peculiar way "normalizes") the outrage Jacob considers the Eisaacic God's trial of faith to be.

One other detail of the Lot story can suggest that Lot is being represented by Jacob as a refiguration of Isaac. When Lot tries to persuade his sons-in-law to leave Sodom, they regard him *kimṣaḥēq*—"as one who jests," as a Yitzchak, an Isaac (19:14). Lot may not be successful in addressing them with prophetic voice, any more than he was successful in addressing the Sodomites the night before in protest against their sexual designs on his guests. But Lot does not hesitate to make his voice heard. He even argues with the angels after he is out of Sodom and they wish to direct him to the hills. "I cannot escape to the mountain lest sickness overcome me and I die" (19:19). Perhaps our present verse 29 retains an old Eisaacic conclusion to the Lot story: "And it came to pass, when God destroyed the cities of the Plain, that God remembered Abraham and sent Lot out from the midst of the upheaval when he overturned the cities that Lot dwelt among." If so, the preceding verses of protest by Lot, in which he asks to be allowed to remain a city dweller, may be read as a protest against the old "mountain story" and its scurrilous history of Moab and Ammon. If the story of Lot's daughters is Jacobic, we can read these mountain events as a refiguration of the seedy business on Mount Moriah: Incest ("let us quicken seed from our father") refigures child sacrifice (the threat to the legitimate seed of Abraham), and the invention of a tale in which other peoples are said to derive from incestuous unions may be a way of exorcising the last nastiness of the Eisaacic trial of faith. In any case, Lot's garrulousness undoes—or at the very least contrasts with—the pious silence of Isaac.

I would like to close this section with an even more than usually speculative thought about two textual difficulties in the Isaac and Lot stories. According to the Masoretic text, in a passage previously examined, the reprieved Abraham lifted his eyes and beheld *ʾayil ʾaḥar*—a ram behind him, or a belated ram, or a ram who is "other" than Isaac (22:13). Although this wonderful phrase may simply represent a scribal error for *'ayil 'eḥād*—the rather pedestrian and unnecessary specification of *a* ram—a ram who is behind Abraham may represent, for Jacob, the religious perspective that looks up to heaven and looks behind events to divine providence. If so, the "ram behind" may be the basis for the famous prohibition, in the Jacobic story of Lot's escape, against looking back. Behold a crux: in the Masoretic text, Lot's wife looks *mē'aḥărâw*—behind him—rather than *mē'aḥărehā*—behind her (19:26). From an Eisaacic viewpoint, she is perhaps guilty of the sin of disobedience; if there is a general prohibition in effect against looking back, it may represent a prohibition against regrets, qualms, reservations. But from a Jacobic perspective, she looks back in violation of the nakedness of the story's origins. To look behind Lot and see Isaac is to lose one's status as character in the tale. Lot's wife steps out of story-time into the timeless realm of the interlunations between texts.

The Overlooking of Isaac

What follows in the narrative sequence after the *'ăqēdâ* is a pair of stories emphasizing human dialogue and human initiative. In place of direct, divine intervention as in the *'ăqēdâ* and Sodom stories, we have two forms of "externalization" of a religious standard. In the first, Abraham turns to meticulously civil (polite and secular) purchase of the land for Sarah's burial plot; the theme of title to the land by divine fiat is thus reworked into the "external" form of possession by public commerce. In the second story, the promptings of the divine are "externalized" as the plottings of Eliezer and the actions of Rebecca. The story of Rebecca has so much of a life of its own that it seems to be imported from another genre and a later time, but in certain ways it weaves an elaborate, Jacobic complement to the Eisaacic story of Sarah's burial.

The exegetical problem "Where is Isaac?" has often tagged 23:3: "Abraham rose up from the presence of his dead and spoke to the children of Heth." Having twice written, "The two of them walked together" in describing Abraham and Isaac on the way to Mount Moriah (22:6, 8), why has Eisaac not given us a picture of Abraham and Isaac together mourning the passing of Sarah? Eisaac portrays Isaac at the center of the stage of Abraham's religious life, but Isaac is conspicuously absent from the domestic scene of the mourning and burial arrangements. Or rather, Eisaac "domesticates" the burial arrangements and leaves Isaac, child of the promise, to matters of the promise. He is treated like a firstborn son dedicated to the priesthood, one who does not soil his hands with burial of the dead or tilling the soil. Perhaps one can say that the Jacobic story of the acquisition of Isaac's wife finds a point of origin in the character of the ghostliest of the three fathers as portrayed by Eisaac: here is a character who will have to be married off by the more practical and energetic members of his household. There is a wonderful midrash about the ethereal and studious Isaac being whisked off by angels at the time of the *ʿăqēdâ* reprieve and living the life of a talmudic student till he is suddenly needed, when Rebecca has ridden her camel to his homesite. The angels hastily convey their otherworldly charge from the academy in Babylon to the field where Rebecca beholds him, "meditating" (either still studying or dizzy from jet lag). In one version, Isaac is so hastily redeposited that he lands headfirst, and it is no wonder that his bride-to-be alights from her camel; she falls off in surprise. In a sense, the seed for such midrash is already sown in the Eisaacic text by the absence of Isaac from the narrative following the *ʿăqēdâ*. Jacob then cultivates such seed in supplying a leisurely tale of the acquisition of Rebecca by proxy.

The story of the *mĕʿārat hammakpēlâ,* the Cave of Couples, leads us, and possibly led Jacob, to the story of the coupling of Isaac. Besides the absence of Isaac, the stories share an important political theme—what it means to be among but not "of" the people. In the Eisaacic story, Abraham declares himself a *gēr,* an alien or "resident stranger" dwelling with the local people but not assimilated with them. They answer him by acknowledging him to be "God's prince in our midst" (23:6), but Abraham moves to acquire a fixed place that will be recognized as a legal transaction by the assembled and their children to come. In the Jacobic story, Abraham and his servant will insist on the special status of living *bĕqirbô* or *bĕʾarṣô,* in the midst (24:3) or in the land (24:37) of the Canaanites. *Qirbô* (its middle) and *qibrô* (its grave) are perhaps too near allied for Abraham's comfort. He wishes to distance himself from the Hittites by owing them no favors and to distance his son from them by owing no marriage ties. In Eisaac's story, the Hittites wish to give Abraham what he wants; in Jacob's story, it is Yava who has given Abraham all he has (24:36); owning only the obligation to God, he owns no other ties. The Eisaacic story is weighed down by the material business of paying for the plot, shekeling each shekel so that not a coin of the transaction nor the significance of its being in coin shall be overlooked (23:16). Abraham's servant weighs out the jewelry for Rebecca (24:23) with no less ceremony or sense of acquisition. But if the lady, like the land, is well paid for, the audience has changed. The Eisaacic story seems to be making a primarily political, or extraliterary, point; the Jacobic story is not international (Hebrew/Hittite) but intertextual (Eisaac/Jacob). There is one point in the Eisaacic story where particular attention is called to the text of utterance: Abraham listens with great attention to the polite response of Efron the Hittite and picks up the number four hundred shekels as the exchange-value of the land (23:16). But the Jacobic story makes listening a leisure activity; the folktale business about a lady so kind she will draw water for man and beast alike is repeated three times. "Where there is leisure for fiction," if one may make a midrashic addition to a famous dictum of Dr. Johnson, "there is little room for politics or grief." It is possible that in the blessing of Rebecca by her brother and mother, there remains something of a political leitmotif: "May your descendants inherit the gates of your enemies" reminds us of the negotiations at the Hittites' city gates in the Eisaacic tale. But on the whole, Jacob replaces both the political concern and the sad constraints of the arrangements for Sarah's burial with the happier freedom of the story of Isaac's betrothal.

Perhaps the most remarkable moment in Jacob's story is the one when Isaac reenters the narrative to be the subject of three active verbs and one passive: "Isaac brought her to the tent of Sarah his mother; he took Rebecca and she was a wife to him; he loved her; Isaac was comforted for his mother" (24:67). The reinhabited tent of Sarah is Jacob's answer to the Eisaacic burial plot. This story, like that one, concludes with a "placing" of sorrow; but in leading us to Sarah's tent in place of Sarah's grave, Jacob leads by the heartstrings, and he leads from death to life.

·5·

JACOB'S BROOD

ANTONIO: This was . . .
A thing not in his power to bring to pass,
But sway'd and fashion'd by the hand of Heaven.
Was this inserted to make interest good?
Or is your gold and silver ewes and rams?

SHYLOCK: I cannot tell; I make it breed as fast.
—Shakespeare, *The Merchant of Venice*

Double Portions

During the Vietnam War, the whores of Saigon would accost American soldiers with the lure, "You number one!" Whether or not the fiction of virginity ("You're my first man") is conventional in such circumstances, the phrase achieved an added poignancy as protesters of the war back home challenged the American presence in Vietnam and the cult of America as "Number One," the policeman of the world and the military power whose *virtu* was infused into the individual man willing to fight. Perhaps the war machine always relies on a version of the "number one" idea, but the alliance of patriotic fervor and appeal to virility was particularly striking when mothers back home and daughters of the camp seemed to be uttering the same words.

I risk beginning this chapter with so scurrilous an example in order to call attention to something scurrilous in the biblical theme of "You Number One." The literary artist who fully believes in the divine selection of the Number One people and its ancestors may have as unproblematic a relation to that jingoistic rallying cry as military leaders or religious fanatics. But for the literary artist as belated mythmaker, inventor of tales of the Number One, there must be some sweet to hide the bitter aftertaste of so deleterious a fiction. Whatever his sources in oral or written history, Eisaac as well as Jacob may be regarded as a literary inventor whose uneasy relationship to the Number One idea served as motive for mythmaking. Perhaps such a remark was unnecessary when we were looking at the stories of Abraham and Isaac, but when we turn to Jacob, we cannot ignore the political dimension of Esau's claim for favor. Eisaac and Jacob both feel the burden of the arbitrariness of the divine choice, though they handle ambivalence about this theme in very different ways.

For Eisaac, the conflict between Jacob and Esau provides another instance of the underdog, the Second who becomes First "by merit raised" to divine choice. Eisaac gives us no predetermination in the womb, and only the barest of character sketches before the crucial story:

> The boys grew, and Esau became a skillful hunter, an outdoorsman; Jacob a man of integrity, a homebody. Now Jacob made a stew, and Esau came from the field exhausted. Esau said to Jacob, "Let me gulp down some of that red stuff; I'm tired!" (That is why he came to be called *'ĕdôm,* "Red.") Jacob said, "How about selling your birthright to me?" Esau answered, "Look, I'm dying [of hunger]; what do I want with a 'birthright'?" Jacob said, "Will you swear to me, right now?" Esau swore and sold his birthright to Jacob. Jacob gave Esau bread and stew; he fed and drank and went on his way. Thus Esau scoffed at the birthright. (25:27, 29–34)

Some scholars of the documentary hypothesis believe that the last verse quoted is part of the E document; if it has the appearance of a belated, moral perspective, we can regard this Eisaacic story as one that is written, or at least retold, from the perspective of the last sentence. The Eisaacic story minimizes the nastiness and suppresses the wiliness of Father Jacob.

It is part of the wiliness of Jacob the writer that in reviewing Eisaac's story of Jacob he should usurp the "birthright" or priority of that story and give to Jacob an "earlier" as well as a more complete triumph. In Jacob's story, Rebecca is the prime mover, the mother par excellence who gives her son the assurance, "You Number One." Jacob pictures Rebecca resorting to divination for help through her difficult pregnancy. What she is told may be as ambiguous as the pronouncements of the Delphic Oracle: "Two nations are in your womb; two peoples will be separated from your bowels; one will be stronger than the other, and the older will subjugate or ['be subjugate to'] the younger." There follow two etymologies Jacobic in their craft: Esau is "Red" because he is red-haired, a phenomenon less significant in itself than in the fact that it challenges the authority of the Eisaacic story of the red stew. Jacob is a "heel" because he emerges from the womb holding his brother's heel. This early narrative concludes with an insertion about the parents' preferences: Isaac loves Esau *kî ṣayid bĕpîw,* a neutral enough description if translated "because he had a predilection for wild game," but a little less savory if translated literally, "he had game in his mouth." (In the sentences about seeking Yava's aid, it is Isaac about whom the verb *wayye'tar* is used [25.21], specifying divination through sacrificial offering whose smell is pleasing to Yava.) Rebecca simply loves Jacob, with no reason given, though one might extrapolate from the placement of this verse right after 27 that *yaʿăqōb ʾîš tām* is understood not in some neutral sense, "Jacob was a simple man," but with the moral connotation, "Jacob was a man of integrity, a 'perfect' man as Noah was said to be 'perfect.'" I think, however, that Jacob's worthiness belongs to the old Eisaacic text, while Rachel's unconditional preference is a Jacobic, domesticated equivalent of pure divine favor.

In Jacob's hands, the story of the birthright becomes the story of paternal benediction. Though the Hebrew *bĕrākâ* (blessing) requires only a flipping of two letters to yield *bĕkōrâ* (birthright), the phonemic near identity is but an emblem of the near identity of meaning. Since we are dealing, in either case, with the abstract concept of favor rather than the measurable distribution of material patrimony, what really is the difference between receiving the blessing or the birthright? The "double portion of spirit" that Elisha requests in conversation with his spiritual father Elijah takes birthright as metaphor for the blessing of election. The real difference is not the meaning but the means—the narrative by which these transfers are recorded. In the Eisaacic story of the sale of the birthright, Esau exclaims, "Behold, I'm on the point of death; what is 'birthright' to me?" The second part of this exclamation, the *lāmmâ-zeh* ("why is it [important to me]?") may be the seed with which Jacob reinseminates the story of Rachel's pregnancy and search for divine aid: *lāmmâ-zeh ʾānōkî* ("Why is it I am ['in life' or 'afflicted']? What am I doing with this agony in my womb?"). But the first part of Esau's exclamation, his hyperbole "I am dying!", becomes the seed of the story of blessing. Now Isaac sees, in a less frivolous sense, that his death is upon him, and it is time to bestow the potent brew of his blessing.

Does Isaac too sell his favor for a mess of porridge? The strange request that Isaac makes of Esau makes it sound as though the blessing must rise not from the "soul" but from the filled belly of the feaster: "Go out to the fields, shoot me some game, and make me a tasty dish—the way I like it. Bring it to me and I will eat—so that my soul will bless you before I die" (27:3–4). It makes most sense if we read the connection between food and favor as Jacob's comment on the connection as found in the Eisaacic story of the birthright. Jacob the Contemplative Man or ectomorph vies with Esau the Active Man or mesomorph for the satisfaction of Isaac's endomorphic appetite. Another way: It is not Esau's muscle that Jacob envies but the flaccidness of the Eisaacic tale that Jacob the writer is determined to harden through the exercise of creative imagination. It would not be right to say that Eisaac is the sort of writer who carelessly confuses spiritual and comestible sustenance, but Jacob misreads Eisaac as being such. It is probably Jacob who inserts, "Isaac loved Esau because of the game in his mouth," and even more probably Jacob who devises a tale in which the old man seems bent on the food itself: "Bring me the dish I love!" (27:4).

Two forms of verbal repetition follow, together complicating or obscuring the sense that the theft of the blessing is a repetition in a finer tone of the sale of the birthright. The first is the literal repetition by Rebecca of Isaac's words. Such leisure for fiction, so gracefully exploited in the story of Eliezer and Rebecca, seems especially appropriate to belated writing with a subtle sense of divine providence. That is, the sense of God working "behind the scenes" licenses the free play of wholly human interactions; Jacob's story need not hasten to its conclusion because there is no threat of overt intervention by Eisaac—or Yava. The other mode of repetition is the reworking of a phrase or a device freed from the constraints of its original context. Here, the Eisaacic injunction to Abraham, *šĕmaʿ bĕqōlāh*—heed her voice!—(21:12) returns as Rebecca's repeated injunction to Jacob: *šĕmaʿ bĕqōlî*—heed my voice! (27:13). Within the story, Jacob's actions have the blessing of divine favor "naturalized" as mother's favoritism; intertextually, Jacob the writer's efforts seem favored by the muse: Jacob's Rebecca seems connected not just with Eisaac's Sarah but with the sources of authority itself. It is not surprising that rabbinic midrash supplies the moral integrity absent from Jacob's Jacob and the sense of pious fulfillment of injunction absent from Jacob's Rebecca; but Jacob's narrative itself functions like a cadenza, an extravagance that wanders far from the morality and pious nationalism of Eisaac's demure tale.

Jacob the character sticks closely to his mother's instructions, displaying if anything less initiative than Eisaac's Jacob, who at least made his own soup. But when Isaac asks Jacob for an explanation for his son's rather remarkable speedy compliance with his wishes, Jacob's own voice colors his ostensibly pious response: *hiqrâ YHWH ʾĕlōhêkâ lĕpānāy* (Yava your God so arranged matters for me, he made it happen "before me," before my very eyes). The verb suggests the same piety that Abraham's servant displayed in 24:12, requesting divine assistance in finding Isaac a wife. Ostensibly, there is a double modesty to Jacob's answer: he attributes his success to God's favor, and he calls Yava his father's god, as though to call him his own would be to usurp the blessing he seeks. But there is also something playfully impudent about thus fitting his tale into the "given" of Isaac's discourse to Esau: "God," Jacob the writer tells Eisaac as Jacob the character tells Isaac, "has given me the perfect set-up."

Reading this extraordinary tale, we do not pause to distinguish the truth of Jacob's voice from the fiction that his arms have the feel of Esau's. What happens instead is that Jacob re-presents the entire physical world to Isaac, compensating for the defective sight—elsewhere so closely allied to divine providence—by affording Isaac the opportunity to feel, taste, touch, and smell. Isaac's blessing seems to well up from this sensory fullness to a something-more-than-nature, as though prophecy were engendered by the reach beyond ordinary experience, beyond ordinary time. Isaac takes in the smell of the field in Jacob's clothes and crosses the sensory divide from what can be to what "must be" possible: "Behold! The smell of my son is like the smell of a field that Yava has blessed!" (27:27). The otherwise innocent expletive *rĕʾēh*—behold—becomes a moment of transcendence for blind Isaac. At this point Isaac does see, but with prophetic sight. The "as if" that makes him leap from the smell of his son to the smell of divine benediction makes him leap as well from facticity to fiat: "May God grant you the dews of the heavens and the fat of the land" becomes a blessing that must stick: God *will* grant you these blessings and more. A few verses later, Isaac tells Esau that the word of Isaac is as inexorable as the word of God: Because I blessed Jacob, "he will be blessed" (27:34)—whether I like it or not.

Because of the various repetitions within the blessing story, many scholars of the documentary hypothesis have concluded that the story we have must be composite. Yet without exception, every repeated element in Isaac's or Rebecca's directives can be explained as Jacobic play, heightening the drama by lingering over its details or capturing an Eisaacic inflection. Nowhere is this possibility of lingering as self-conscious fiction-making better exploited than at the moment of blessing itself:

> [Isaac] did not recognize him because his hands were like the hands of Esau his brother, hairy; [Isaac] blessed him. [Isaac] said, "Are you Esau my son?" [Jacob] answered, "I am." [Isaac] said, "Draw near, I will eat from my son's stew so that my soul will bless you." [Jacob] served him, [Isaac] ate, [Jacob] brought wine, [Isaac] drank. Isaac his father said to him, "Come close and kiss me, my son!" [Jacob] drew near and kissed him; [Isaac] smelled the smell of [Jacob's] garments and blessed him. He said, "Behold, the smell of my son is like the smell of a field that Yava has blessed. May God grant you [from his foison] the dews of the heavens and the fat of the land. . . ." (27:24–28)

If this passage shows the hand of a redactor, it is Jacob the redactor, teasing us with a blessing that is announced but put off for one more assurance. In the blessing itself, however, the first line (behold . . .) seems to come like an afterthought of a different origin from what follows it. That is, "May God grant you" (and it is Elohim, Eisaac's god who is specified) seems to begin an already inscribed blessing, as though Isaac had this family relic to hand down, while the invocation of the field that has Yava's blessing appears to be a new thought, a spontaneous thought added to an old script. If it is correct to see the entire blessing scene as original with Jacob, then the story is really a supreme scene of instruction between Isaac/Eisaac and Jacob/Jacob: The sense we have that the blessing proper is an old Eisaacic formula capped by a Jacobic introduction only summarizes the effect of the whole tale of mingling the indelibility of old Isaacic/Eisaacic words with the verve of Jacobic originality.

Were Jacob more of a benign moralist, content to be Number Two in the school of Eisaac, perhaps he would have been content to have Isaac represented as blessing his son with the fat of the land without going on to specify the purchase of this blessing at a brother's expense. It is a blessed child indeed whose parent can convey unlimited love without needing to denigrate siblings to make the child in question feel special. But Jacob the writer has Isaac the patriarch go on to specify, "May various peoples serve you and nations bow down to you; may you have the upper hand over your brother and may your mother's sons bow down to you." This is "You Number One" with some of the sordid, bellicose nationalism that has attached itself to the "chosen people" idea. Jacob's trick, however, is to pass off the nastier part of the blessing as though it were Eisaacic lore, and the invention of Isaac the patriarch—just as the idea of the theft belongs to Rebecca the matriarch, not to her son and the people he comes to represent.

In the narrative that follows, Isaac sticks to the concept of exclusive blessing while Esau cries out for a more liberal interpretation: "Bless me too, father!" (27:34). Though our national interest pits us with Jacob against Esau—one necessarily reads Genesis as an Israelite, just as one ostensibly reads *The Iliad* as a Greek—our literary interest, our human sympathies, are with Esau versus Jacob. But so well crafted is this story that we sense the outcry as that not of brother against brother but child against parent. Our sympathies, that is, are with Jacob's Esau as against Isaac/Eisaac's inexorability.

Isaac speaks of the blessing as something given and consumed once and for all, like a single portion of stew, but Esau repeats and elaborates his plea, arguing that it is altogether unfair that Jacob should be capable of a double deception (birthright and blessing) while Isaac can only come up with a single blessing: "Do you really have only one blessing, my father? Bless me too, my father!" (27:38). Here the Septuagint preserves a wonderful, Jacobic pause: "Isaac was silent." Perhaps the line dropped out of the Masoretic text not because it was short and easy to skip over but because it represents too much a Jacobic achievement at the expense of Eisaacic piety. Isaac silent and Esau weeping—it is a moment of uncovering the nakedness of fathers, a scene (like that of Keats's Saturn and Mnemosyne) from which an Eisaacic scribe might well avert his eyes. In the pathos of this moment it seems as if not just the blessing-power of

Isaac the character but the seminal nature of Eisaacic narrative is being called into question. When Isaac speaks again he has made room for Esau—not extratextually, in the space of Canaanite geography, but intratextually, in the space of a Jacobic pun. Jacob had received the blessing, "May God grant you . . . *mišmannê hā'āreṣ* (from the fat of the land)." Now Isaac repeats the phrase but with a revised meaning of "from": You will not receive *a part* of these boons but a boon *apart,* [far] from the dew of the land and the fat of the earth. Though both blessings are mouthed by a character I believe to be Jacob's Isaac, the story is so written as to present the former as a blessing of an Eisaacic Isaac, maker of a mistake, while the latter is the blessing of a Jacobic Isaac, wily discoverer of a way out. Jacob's answer to Esau's complaint is represented first as geographic distance: Jacob will enjoy the blessings from (deriving from) the land; you will enjoy blessings from (away from) the land God is giving the Children of Jacob. This distance is then doubled as temporal distance: You will serve your brother and live at war—that much is given, but add:—*for a while.* Then you will shake his yoke from your neck.

There is one further compensation to Esau that mollifies the aftertaste of the draft of "Number One" poured out for Jacob. Even the prophecy of Jacob's supremacy and enjoyment of Canaan has to be put off; in the interim, the supremacy and exclusive enjoyment of the land are Esau's. According to the old Eisaacic account (27:46–28:5), Jacob goes to his father's kinsfolk, at Isaac's bidding, to seek a wife. In the new Jacobic myth, Jacob flees the wrath of Esau, and he flees at his mother's initiative, to return, she specifies, when she calls for him. Although that particular moment of anticipated control will never come to be, Esau will be further reworked, in the hands of Jacob the writer, into a character surprisingly sympathetic and human, if not "godlike." In the interim, Rebecca remains the most Jacobic of the mothers: Her strong will in conflict with Isaac's deflects critical attention from the strong will of Jacob the writer in the struggle with his precursor Eisaac.

Upstairs, Downstairs at Beth-el

The brief narrative of Jacob's night stop at Beth-el, on his way to Haran, has occasioned a host of rabbinic midrashim that fill in the silences of the biblical text and supply Priestly connections to preceding events and to the subsequent religious history of the people. There are simple stories of the stones at Jacob's head coming from the *'ăqēdâ* altar, and there are complex explanations of how the site that Jacob names Beth-el, ostensibly a town distinct from Jerusalem, gets to be the Temple after all. Most of this material seems more pious, more normative, than the vision in

Jacob's dream, and reading it one can capture something of the special challenge that must have met Jacob in the bare, Eisaacic account.

Of what did such an account consist? Let us continue to suppose that the Eisaacic text is preserved within the text as we have it, and that the phrases scholars have singled out as marking a redactor's shift to a J text mark, rather, Jacobic insertions into a text previously without comparable material. Eisaac's story would look like this:

> Jacob left Beer-sheba and journeyed toward Haran. He stumbled upon The Place and stopped there, for the sun was setting. He took from the stones of The Place, and putting one by his head, he went to sleep in That Place. He dreamt—and lo, a staircase set on the earth with its top reaching the heavens. Behold: angels of God are ascending and descending it.
>
> He was afraid. He exclaimed, "How awesome is This Place! Surely this [ziggurat?] is the House of God, and this [stair?] is the Gate of Heaven!"
>
> Jacob rose early in the morning. He took the stone that he had placed by his head and erected it as a monument. He anointed it with oil, and called the name of the place *bêt-ʾēl* (House of God). Jacob made a vow: "If God will be with me, will guard me in this way that I am going, and [if] I return in peace to my father's house, this stone that I have erected as a monument will be a house of God; I will tithe for you everything you give me." (28:10–12, 17–18, 19a, 20–21a, 22)

It is impossible to translate this beautiful passage without confronting some of its most problematic features. A *māqôm* can be just an ordinary place, but it can also mean "special place" or "religious site," perhaps evoking specifically the place Abraham saw as the appointed one for the *ʿăqēdâ*. The verb beginning verse 11 may be neutrally translated "reached" ("Jacob reached a certain place")—but it has special connotations of encounter, as though the meaning of the passage were tied to the reader's ability to perceive a special encounter before we actually get to it. Thus the episode begins with suggestive ambiguity about how strong a hand Providence is playing. There is a similar problem about *bêt-ʾēl:* Should one translate *bêt* literally as "house," or figuratively as "place"? Is Jacob pointing to the building he saw in his dream, the ziggurat of the mind, when he says "this is *bêt-ʾēl,*" or is he meditating on the sanctity of the geographical spot? The way one answers such a question affects the tone of the whole passage as Priestly (in the sense of privileging the earthly House of Worship) or Elohistic (evoking the pure transcendence of a deity most present when seemingly most distant). Finally, and perhaps most naggingly, there is the question of the conditional nature of the vow. I have followed standard documentary procedure in deleting the phrase "then Yava will be my God," which we assume to be Jacobic, but I have also deleted further conditions: "If God will be with me, will guard me in this way I am going, *and will give me bread to eat, and clothes to wear.*" Whether or not I am correct to suppose these words a Jacobic addition, there is something strange about the verb that immediately follows them: *wěšabtî* means "I will return," not "You will bring me back." We can supply the wish "*if* I return in peace," or we can accentuate the conditional nature of the devotion promised by translating, "If God will be with me . . . *so that* I return in peace." The problem in translation points to the larger question of how much initiative, as opposed to modest piety, Jacob is exhibiting.

Like the staircase of Jacob's vision, which leads both up and down, the pathways between texts allow for descents as well as ascents from early to revised version. Although it is the argument of this book that a consistent personality can be descried behind the Jacobic, it is not an argument of this book that the Jacobic is necessarily an "improvement" on the Eisaacic. In considering the story of the *ʿăqēdâ,* for example, we encountered an Eisaacic text of such purity and clarity that the Jacobic second epiphany tagged onto it could only be interpreted as weak-minded chiming in—if it is not a "backstair," leading surreptitiously to a doctrine wholly undermining the primary text. I do not have a similarly explosive possibility to propose for the story of Jacob's dream, but I do see the challenge of the Eisaacic story of Jacob's dream to be somewhat analogous to that of the *ʿăqēdâ.*

What is that challenge? The most remarkable feature of Jacob's dream vision is its silence. In Eisaac's story, Jacob sees the ziggurat, but he hears nothing. Yet because we know how emotionally charged is Father Jacob's departure from Canaan, *we* hear, or think we hear, intimations about Jacob's mobility in the words that picture the mobility of the angels. The angelic staircase thus seems to function in Eisaac's vision like Ezekiel's vision of the divine chariot. And just as Ezekiel points to the *miqdāš mĕʿaṭ,* the "little sanctuary" (11:16) that will symbolize the Divine Presence outside the land of Canaan, Eisaac points to the *bêt-ʾel,* or heavenly house that is not to be identified with a single, holy, geographic place. Now it is a curious feature of the textual history of Ezekiel's vision that just the words proclaiming the visual mobility of the chariot should have come down to us, in the Masoretic text, altered so as to proclaim a heavenly utterance: In place of *bĕrûm kĕbôd-YHWH mimmĕqômô* (when the Glory of Yava was ascending from its place), we have *bārûk kĕbôd* . . . ([angels proclaiming,] "*Blessed* be the Glory of Yava from His place!" 3:12). The Masoretic text supplies (by a misprinting of one letter) the "blessed," and rabbinic interpretation adds the angels proclaiming this benediction. If this is scribal error, it is an error so consistent with the pious impulse to utter God's praises as to have justly become a familiar liturgical formula, centerpiece of the Jewish Sanctification Service. We need not attribute liturgical motives to Jacob in "voicing" the silent vision of Eisaac, but if the resulting passage is a little too normatively pious to sound like Jacob, creator of *unheimlich* midrashim, we may still be able to recognize in the Eisaacic vision a silence Jacob found particularly threatening.

In place of the standard documentary hypothesis, which features a redactor quoting an E text for the vision and shifting to a J text for the speech of God within that vision, we can suppose the Eisaacic text to be vision and vision only, broken into by Jacob with an untimely rent. Eisaac's story pictures Father Jacob erecting a *maṣēbâ,* a pillar or monument that will mark the spot of the dream vision until Jacob can return and build a religious sanctuary. But Jacob's "constructions" are of a different order, and we might hear in the word *maṣṣēbâ* the root *nṣb,* which becomes the basis of the extraordinary interference in Eisaac's dream vision, the appearance of Yava *niṣṣab ʿālāyw* (literally "on him" or "above him," but understood idiomatically to mean "beside him"). The verb comes from a root that means to stand or to take a stand, and it represents not just Yava taking a stand beside Jacob but Jacob the writer taking a stand "over and against" Eisaac's dream vision. Yava does not "fit into" that vision. He might be thought to be standing at the top rung (as in King James); but he is, in any case, a preemptor, one who destroys the transcendent silence of Jacob's vision to proclaim, before Eisaac's Jacob can wake and proclaim, the freedom of God from fixed place.

With Jacob's additions, Eisaac's story is twice preempted. First, and most boldly, there is the Jacobic revision of the vow into divine proclamation. Eisaac's Jacob had said, *ʾim yihyeh ʾĕlōhîm ʿimmādî,* "If God will be with me . . ." (28:20). Jacob's Yava proclaims, *ʾānōkî ʿimmāk,* "I am with you!" (28:15). Without the speech of Yava, Jacob's vow represents Eisaacic transcendence in the form of delicate and accurate "reading" of the vision: When Jacob says "if God will be with me," he is showing his mastery of the "content" of the vision, its symbolism of God's abiding presence with him, wherever he goes. But with the speech of Yava, Jacob's vow looks much less like a "reading" than a vow, a much-diminished thing from an Eisaacic point of view, though it simultaneously increases the agonistic or strong-willed character of Jacob. This last point is all the stronger if we can suppose that Jacob the writer adds to the vow the specifications "keep me in this way that I go *and give me bread to eat and clothes to wear.*" In any event, Jacob the writer appears to add the outrageous bargaining term "Yava will be my God." Ostensibly, Jacob is simply asserting that he looks forward to the return to Canaan and the worship of Yava in this place; but if the figurative meaning of "Yava will be my God" is "I will duly worship him then," the literal meaning has all the force of a Jacobic reversal of Eisaacic meaning. Instead of a vow that means "I know God will be with me and I promise to worship him properly," we have one that casts divine mobility in question: "*If* God will fill the following conditions, *I* will grant him the status of 'my God.'"

The other preemption may be interpreted as a minor version of the one just examined. In the Eisaacic text, Jacob greets his vision with the terror appropriate to the sublime: "He exclaimed, 'How awesome is this place!'" But Jacob the writer inserts, for his character and for himself, something in a different tone: "Jacob awakened from his sleep and said, 'So . . . Yava is in this place. And I didn't know it!'" The sublime is prevented by the curious.

If it is correct thus to read the "J fragments" as Jacobic additions, our author/redactor has certainly altered the total effect of the tale. The lofty vision of divine mobility seems rather a contrast with than a concomitant of Jacob's horizontal mobility. The vision is not wholly rewritten or undermined, but it is "put in its place." Eisaac's Jacob goes off to Haran with a wily revisionist ever at his heel.

The Eisaacic dream and vow at Beth-el come up twice more, once in 35:7, which seems to refer to the angels of the visionary staircase as *'ĕlōhîm,* and once in 31:13, where the question of just what is the text may depend on whether or not one accepts the argument for a belated Jacobic revisionist. The Masoretic text reads, *'ānōkî hā'ēl bêt-'ēl,* "I am the God [of] Beth-el," while the Aramaic Targum and the Septuagint translate as though the Hebrew read, *'ānōkî hā'ēl hannir'eh 'ēleykā bĕbêt-'ēl,* "I am the God who revealed himself to you at Beth-el." These translations may preserve a phrase that has dropped out of the Masoretic text, a phrase that would tend to point to an Eisaacic text of the Beth-el episode that included verbal revelation from God. But I believe, rather, that the translations are *supplying* a phrase based on their understanding of the Beth-el episode as univocal. As an Eisaacic text, chapter 31 refers to Beth-el with no mention of a Yava-revelation; Eisaac knows of it only as a place of Jacob's dream and Jacob's vow. Of course Jacob the writer or a Jacobic editor could have inserted the phrase in question into verse 13, just as verse 3, a characteristic Jacobic reworking, has been added to the Eisaacic account. But if it is correct to read the Masoretic text of 31:13 as it stands, then we can see the translators' instinct as informed by their awareness of the text of chapter 28 as we have it, with the Jacobic reshaping.

Laban's Usage

Eisaac's Jacob goes to Haran to fulfill his father's injunction to select a wife from his mother's family. Shaping the Haran material, Eisaac is motivated by the desire to show Jacob as mature and pious as possible. The youthful

Jacob who coaxed his brother into betraying his birthright must emerge as Father Jacob, wise, patient, and just, with a partiality—but not a reprehensible partiality—for Rachel. Eisaac's goal can be represented in the birth of the child Rachel calls *Joseph,* from the root *'sp,* "to remove." With the birth of Joseph, a cloak of dishonor is removed from Rachel and she becomes not just a literal mother but a figure "remembered" by God (as Noah was remembered); she becomes a matriarch. At the same time, the last stains of dishonor are removed from Jacob, and he is ready to return to Canaan doubly wived and richly blessed by God with wealth that has providentially and legitimately come to be his.

But there is a second etymology of the name Joseph, from the verb *ysp,* "to add." When Rachel calls her son "Give me another!" she represents not the Eisaacic sublimity of character transcending reproach but the Jacobic, all-too-human female in rivalry with her sister. Perhaps we can therefore allow this second etymology to represent the conflicting goals of the Jacobic narrative. If Father Jacob (in the Eisaacic narrative) prefers Rachel, Jacob the writer prefers Leah; if the Eisaacic Jacob grows in respectability at Haran, the Jacobic Jacob grows in wiliness. Student of his trickster mother in the business of the paternal blessing, this Jacob finds his mettle more severely tested by his mother's kind, her trickster brother. He emerges from Haran as *polytropos* (many turning) as Odysseus, ready to take on man or god.

The Eisaacic account of Jacob's adventures in Haran may have begun with some decorous offer on Jacob's part to work for his board. It seems that the portion of the Eisaacic account preserved for us begins with the words "When Jacob had stayed with Laban for a month, Laban said to Jacob, 'Because you are my brother, should you work for nothing?'" (29:14b, 15). The verses that follow appear to introduce Laban's daughters for the first time; in any event they arrange for Jacob's selection of Rachel as the object of his toil. What inspired Jacob the revisionist to add a prevenient account of Father Jacob's meeting Rachel by the well? Let us suppose that the metaphysical *'sp,* the "gathering [of Rachel's disgrace] from off of her"—so Eisaacic a notion—suggested to Jacob a play on words, something (to borrow Wallace Stevens's subtly serpentine phrase) "to roll / On the expressive tongue, the finding fang." If so, we may behold in a pun the germ of a narrative about shepherds who must "gather together" collectively to roll away the stone from the well. In Joshua, Yava says he "rolls away" the shame of Egypt with the new circumcision (5:9), but in Genesis, Jacob merely "rolls away" the stone. This secular action re-presents the physical before the metaphysical: Jacob must be a weight lifter as well as a wrestler, physically, muscularly, *there.*

The hypothesis of such a "source" must be pure fancy; yet it can represent a reaction on the part of Jacob the writer that, I believe, is real. The forefather who rolls that stone, waters Rachel's sheep, and slaps a kiss on her brow is a far cry from the one who meditates in the field while his servant does the well scene and his wife-to-be does the watering. It is the distance of Eisaac to Jacob. Jacob the writer may have written both well scenes, but he has invented or reshaped old material so as to emphasize a fundamental difference in character.

The account of the birth of Jacob's children (29:30–30:24) is mostly Jacobic, with just enough Eisaacic material (30:1–3, 17–20, 21–23) for us to see how much less flattering to Leah Eisaac's account was. The etymologies of *Issachar* and *Zebulun* show a preoccupation with the rivalry hardly different in kind from Rachel's, but those in Jacob's own hand attribute to Leah a piety and a pathos different in kind from anything preserved about Rachel. Even the story of the mandrakes, which seems (if one can judge from the double etymology of *Issachar*) to have had an Eisaacic pre-text, emerges as a story less flattering to Rachel. It may be Leah's Reuben who found the mandrakes, but it is Rachel who must have them. Popular tradition has always maintained that the mandrakes must have been regarded as a fertility drug, and that Rachel asks for *some* of the mandrakes, so that the text implies that Leah uses them to good effect while Rachel tries in vain, presumably the following night. But since we do not hear of Rachel's use of the mandrakes, they remain a mystery suggestive of black magic—a shadow Jacob the writer may have especially wished to cast on Rachel. As we have it, the narrative goes on to specify "God heard Leah" (30:17), thus removing any taint from Leah's ability to attract Jacob or to prove fertile that night. We may have an instance where Jacob wished to have the text proceed precisely with Elohim, Eisaac's god at this point, so as to reaffirm the traditional piety of Leah's actions, whatever it is that Rachel has in mind.

If Jacob the character works long and hard as a shepherd tending Laban's flocks, Jacob the writer proves most aggressive in reworking the account of that shepherding. When Jacob asks permission to gather his wives and children and return to Canaan, Laban entreats him to name his wage and stay on. Jacob proposes a modest wage—that the mutant sheep and goats born from this point on be his: "Pass through the flock today and remove from thence every spotted or speckled [goat], every dark sheep; every spotted or speckled goat [that will be born thereafter, and every dark sheep] will be my wages." This is a conjectural restoration of 30:32, assuming that what Laban goes on to do in verses 35–36 constitutes a fulfillment, rather than a violation, of the agreed-upon plan. If we trust the Eisaacic version that Jacob recounts to Rachel and Leah (31:4–16), the terms of the agreement shift repeatedly, and God makes

Jacob prosper regardless of the way in which Laban rearranges the division.

In tampering with the text, Jacob the revisionist represents Father Jacob tampering with the flock. The passage is worth quoting in Shylock's paraphrase:

> When Laban and himself were compromis'd
> That all the eanlings which were streak'd and pied
> Should fall as Jacob's hire, the ewes, being rank,
> In end of autumn turnèd to the rams,
> And, when the work of generation was
> Between these woolly breeders in the act,
> The skilful shepherd pill'd me certain wands
> And, in the doing of the deed of kind,
> He stuck them up before the fulsome ewes,
> Who then conceiving did in eaning time
> Fall parti-colour'd lambs, and those were Jacob's.
> This was a way to thrive, and he was blest;
> And thrift is blessing, if men steal it not.
> (*The Merchant of Venice,* I.iii.79–91)

By a wonderful coincidence of idiomatic speech and character portrayal, Shylock's "pill'd me" identifies Jacob and Shylock just at the point of tampering with "the deed of kind." Perhaps it is worth calling the revisionist writer of Genesis *Jacob* just so we can picture him inserting into the Eisaacic account this outrageous story of Jacob the character pilling certain rods not only for himself but for his namesake. Shylock's Jacobic character is represented by his ability not only to make gold and silver breed as fast as the character Jacob's ewes and rams, but to make others' words bear interest. Antonio says of interest, "I do never use it," offering Shylock the opportunity to insert the Genesis tale on the strength of the use/ewes pun. Antonio plays Eisaac to Shylock's Jacob, and he reacts to Shylock's tale as Eisaac would respond to the Jacobic midrash:

> This was a venture, sir, that Jacob serv'd for;
> A thing not in his power to bring to pass,
> But sway'd and fashion'd by the hand of heaven.

Antonio is a pure-hearted but misguided interpreter. From Eisaac's perspective, all is "fashion'd by the hand of Heaven," but when Jacob pills those wands for himself, he is not waiting for providential magic. It is Jacob's hand, not the hand of heaven (or Esau) that pulls the wool over Eisaac's eyes.

Keeping the Teraphim

Although the ascription of verses to E and J in the Haran episode is notoriously problematic for documentary scholars, the general opinion is that the story of the teraphim comes from the hand of E. There is some philological reason. At least one E tag, the word *'āmâ* for maidservant, occurs within the teraphim passage (at 31:33). But the ascription to E is founded much more on a sense of doublets and contradictions. For example, in 31:17 Jacob gets up and leaves, and in verse 20 he appears to steal away. If one resolves this difficulty by attributing verse 20 to E, then verse 19, mentioning the teraphim, seems to belong also to E. Similarly, in verse 28 Laban accuses Jacob of stealing the teraphim, but in verse 31 Jacob answers a question posed in verse 27. If one resolves this difficulty by labeling verses 27 and 31 J, then the intervening verses, with the mention of the teraphim, are assignable to E. To justify the ascription of such an episode to E, documentary scholars have had to turn stealing the teraphim into some form of sweetness and light. Since E usually speaks well of everyone possible, Rachel must have been doing something pious or brave. If she were not acting to keep her father from his wicked idolatry (a rabbinic view), she was helping secure for her husband the tokens of his legitimate right to Laban's fortune (E. A. Speiser). I am particularly fond of Speiser's rationalization for translating 31:19, "Rachel meanwhile had appropriated her father's household images":

> A reasonably precise translation is especially important in this instance. The issue is bound up with the purpose of Rachel's act. If it was inspired by no more than a whim, or resentment, or greed, then Rachel stole the images. But if she meant thereby to undo what she regarded as a wrong . . . and thus took the law, as she saw it, into her own hands, the translation "stole" would be not only inadequate but misleading.

One does not need to be a modern lawyer to understand the value of "appropriating" as opposed to "stealing"; it suffices Speiser to know the Nuzi documents and something about Hurrian law. A less erudite, or at least an older, explanation had Rachel concerned not about property rights but about Laban's access, through divination, to information about Jacob's flight. If the teraphim are seraphim, images of angels consulted by astrologers, then Rachel is again acting on her husband's behalf against her father, though now by outwitting his astrologers rather than his lawyers.

These scholarly explanations may seem a far cry from the rabbinic flights of fancy about the nature of the teraphim. (Consider just one: According to the Pirke d'Rabbi Eliezer, the teraphim are the decapitated and salted heads of firstborn men with the names of demons under their tongues.) In general, however, the old rabbis and the modern scholars share both a fascination with the teraphim as objects and a desire to read Rachel's action as laudatory. The impulse to explain the teraphim per se may be Jacobic, but the impulse to explain Rachel's action is Eisaacic. Yet we cannot conclude, from a glance at the exegesis of the text, that the text itself is Eisaacic; on the contrary, it may be the very strength of the Jacobic spirit of the teraphim episode that has produced so fertile an antithetical, Eisaacic reaction.

The teraphim are generally understood to be instruments for divination or idolatry. Discussions of the teraphim seldom include the term *sorcery,* which would imply black magic (appeal to an evil, not just an alien, spirit), and to the best of my knowledge never include the term *witchcraft,* which generally connotes malicious psychic influence over others without (or transcending) reliance on cultic objects like teraphim. And yet there is something in the teraphim incident like the concern about witchcraft—the concern about accusation that transcends concern about the actual power or possession. Witchcraft, as the anthropologist James L. Brain has shown, is among semi-mobile tribes that nasty practice of the *other* tribe, or of that individual one wishes to malign as "other." In our enlightened age, when we burn only the pockets or reputations of those we hate, we might invoke that other dark art read back into Rachel's actions by Speiser—the law—but in ancient times one simply accused one's enemy of being a witch—of having recourse, in the more usual language of the Bible, to foreign gods. Now the most striking thing about Rachel's theft of her father's gods is not that she removes them from his possession but that she appropriates them for her own. Some have made the gracious theological reflection that by sitting on foreign gods while menstruating, Rachel sums up Israelite opinion about other deities. Yet she is not menstruating; she is deceiving her husband as well as her father, and there is no passage detailing her destruction of the images or her revelation of them to Jacob.

Who wants to accuse Rachel of being a witch? Not Eisaac, for whom she is the spotless and true wife of a spotless and true Jacob—*Father* Jacob. Not Jacob the writer, at least not openly. Jacob's Cain is (I have suggested) ordered by Yava to sit there, crouched before but not in sin. Rachel is not taking orders from anyone, but she too just sits there, defying both her father and her husband's vow of death to the offender. If we view her with Eisaacic eyes, her defiance has to be reinterpreted as care in a righteous cause; but if we view teraphim-bearing Rachel as a Jacobic creation, she emerges as an emblem of defiance of the very piety, the very purity, of the story in which she was placed.

That Eisaacic story featured a blameless Jacob, a flawless Rachel and Leah, and a Laban more to be pitied than judged. What can a man do when Providence is against him? Laban turns from bargain to bargain, like the man pursued by Death who runs to the very city where the Angel of Death has been told to find him. Whatever Laban does, Jacob miraculously prospers. Beholding the gloom in Laban's face, Jacob calls his wives and so beautifully narrates his tale of favor at the hands of God, maltreatment at the hand of their father, that the women unhesitatingly assure him of their devotion and support. The story then announces the theme of Jacob's flight (31:17–18) and pauses to detail it:

> Laban went to shear his sheep. Jacob broke the heart of Laban the Aramean because he did not tell him he was fleeing. He—and all that was his—fled, crossed the river, and headed to Mount Gilead. On the third day, Laban heard that Jacob had fled. [Laban] took his brothers with him and pursued [Jacob] for seven days, catching up with him in Mount Gilead.
>
> God came to Laban in a dream at night and said to him, "Watch yourself! Do not let your sweet speech to Jacob turn sour!"
>
> Laban approached Jacob when Jacob had pitched his tent on the mountain; Laban too pitched his tent on Mount Gilead.
>
> Laban said to Jacob: "What did you do? You broke my heart! You carried away my daughters as though they were captives of the sword. Why did you flee secretly, *stealing from me,* and not telling me so that I could send you away in joy, in song, with tambourine and harp? You did not permit me to kiss my grandchildren and my daughters. This was so senseless! I have the strength of hand to do you evil, but the god of your fathers spoke to me last night, saying, 'Watch yourself! Do not let your sweet speech to Jacob turn sour!' And now you are gone—gone! You must have longed so for your father's house!"
>
> Jacob answered Laban and said, "[I fled secretly because] I was afraid. I thought you would seize your daughters from me. What is my sin, what is my transgression, that you should have so pursued me? It has been twenty years that I have been with you, and your ewes and she-goats have not miscarried, nor have I eaten from the rams of your flock. I never brought you [your sheep] home, dead prey of wild animals; I bore the loss, whether [the loss was] a night theft or a day theft. I was scorched by day and frozen by night; sleep fled from my eyes. . . . God saw my affliction and what was due my labors, and he gave judgment last night." (31:19a, 20–30a, 31, 36b–42)

Such might have been the text before the Jacobic addition of the midrash about teraphim. In this idiomatic translation, I have lost the force of *wayyignōb yaʿăqōb ʾet-lēb lābān,* literally "Jacob stole Laban's heart" (31:20), though most translators understand the heart to be the ancient seat of the intellect, so that the sentence describes Jacob deceiving Laban rather than causing him emotional pain. I have opted for the possibility of reading the heart as the seat of the affections in order to emphasize the Eisaacic pathos of the scene, the possibility that Laban indeed acts (or partly acts, for the split marks the combination of Eisaacic pathos and sophistication) from the motives he sets forth to Jacob. The word on which the Eisaacic text dwells is *lēb,* the tender heart that is part of the name and nature of Laban, and perhaps it is just to his own broken heart that Laban is pointing in verse 27 when he questions Jacob's hardheartedness. But the idiom, however it should be translated, also contains the crucial term *wayyignōb,* Jacob "stole," regardless of whether it is the rational judgment (through deception) or the heart's affections (through discourtesy) that Jacob is stealing. Either of these emphasizes the Eisaacic, metaphysical nature of the idiomatic theft. But perhaps no verse so accentuates the metaphor of theft as Laban's cry in verse 27: *stealing from me* is idiomatic English, but *wattignōb ʾōtî* ("stealing me," with a direct object) may be peculiar enough to constitute an "opening" for Jacobic imagination.

Jacob the revisionist steals into this beautiful house of Eisaacic pathos through the shattered window of an idiom. Just before "Jacob broke the heart (or stole the heart) of Laban," Jacob the revisionist adds, "Rachel stole the teraphim that were her father's." Now in Eisaac's story, Laban's pathetic lament to Jacob poses a single, though elaborated question: "Why did you flee secretly, stealing from me?" To this, Jacob the revisionist now adds a second question: "Why did you steal my gods?" (31:30). Eisaacic Jacob begins to respond, "I was afraid. I thought you would seize your daughters from me"—and here the text is rent for the insertion of Jacob's response to the new charge against him:

> "With whomever you find your gods—[that person] shall not live; before our family identify for yourself what is [yours and] with me. Take it!" Now Jacob did not know that Rachel had stolen them. Laban came into Jacob's tent, and into Leah's tent, and into the tent of the two maidservants, and he did not find [them].

At this point, the documentarians make their find: The word for "maidservants" is *ʾămāhōt,* an E word. The story of the teraphim must therefore be an E text, and the fragments of the enveloping story of the Jacob-Laban confrontation must be J. But to such reasoning we can object that the word *tigzōl* in verse 31 (lest you *steal* your daughters from me) is a characteristically E term, and if Jacob's two responses to Laban's questions come from two strands, the first response about figurative theft might be Eisaacic material while the second response, and the remainder of the tale of the teraphim, could be Jacobic. The case for such attributions is strengthened by the peculiarity of the narrative at the point we interrupted it. Laban came into Jacob's tent, and into Leah's tent, and into the maidservants' tent. We expect him to go thence to Rachel's tent, but the verse continues, "He left Leah's tent and entered Rachel's tent." Now we can imagine, in the mode of medieval midrash, a Laban so suspicious of Rachel that he repeatedly returns to her tent in the course of searching through others. But it seems more likely that Jacob the writer did not bother about the maidservants, and pictured Laban searching Jacob's tent, Leah's tent, and Rachel's tent, the story reaching its climax, like a joke told with good economy, in the third effort. If a later hand, meddlesomely extending the sweep of Laban's scrutiny through the tent of the maidservants, added the term *'ămāhōt,* there is no philological case against the ascription of the entire teraphim story to Jacob. The occurrence of the J idiom *'ădōnî* in Rachel's pleading with her father (31:35) is another thread of evidence. But the real magic in the web of the Jacobic yarn interwoven with the Eisaacic tale concerns the technical innocence of Jacob the forefather. It is not the integrity of Eisaac's Jacob but the pathos of Eisaac's story that is complicated or undermined by Jacobic tinkering with just how much and what kind of stealing took place. The "witchcraft" of which Jacob the writer accuses Rachel is his own interest in the dark ways of language—and the heart.

If the depiction of Laban as a character of pathos as well as craft proved particularly alluring or threatening to Jacob the writer, we can imagine him standing with Father Jacob, regarding with uneasiness the changing face of Laban. Whether or not it is correct to suppose the story of the teraphim to be midrashic response to a threat posed by such a fine, Eisaacic portion, we can probably regard as more typical, or more low-key, Jacobic response to Eisaacic greatness, the insertion of the command from Yava to get back to Canaan (31:3). For Jacob the writer, Laban's face is a motive for myth too powerful not to cover with more direct divine command, if not with more direct theft. But for all the "covering," Laban's face remains, for Jacob the writer, a re-presentation of Esau's face. Both are ghastly countenances, haunting images because of the black that orthodox myth has smeared over them, but more haunting for Jacob because of the tears of pathos that the Eisaacic account has too brilliantly portrayed smearing and defying that facade of blackness. In pursuit of (or "from") such images, the following set of narratives derive their power.

Striving with God

The set of passages that culminate with Jacob's reception by Esau has proven particularly difficult to documentary scholars wishing to rely on philological evidence. There is too much confusion, too much doubling of phrase and episode for a simple univocality, but every "paragraph," if not every sentence, seems too replete with J phrases for any clear identification of the hand of E. The sole exception is the introductory setting of the scene:

> Laban rose early the next morning, kissed his grandchildren and his daughters, blessed them, and returned to his place. Messengers of God confronted Jacob as he went on his way. When Jacob saw them he said, "This is God's camp!" He called the place *maḥănāyim*, "twin camps." (32:1–3, English 31:55–32:2. Subtract 1 for subsequent English verse numbers in chapter 32.)

I have unconventionally (and improperly) translated *mal'ākîm* as "messengers" rather than angels in order to call attention to the possibility of a pun—two meanings competing for the same space—in order, that is, to suggest how the opportunity to give space to the two meanings in this clearly Eisaacic text might be regarded as a Jacobic *trouvé*. In the absence of clear philological evidence, I want to speculate on how the two ambiguous terms, *mal'ākîm* and *maḥănāyim*, might have served as points of origin for important Jacobic midrashim.

Let us suppose that the Eisaacic text once continued, after the naming of the place in verse 3, with what we now have as verse 14a: "He passed the night there." The text might then have continued with a version of what we have preserved in verses 14b–22, concluding with Father Jacob still in the same place, but having extended the distance (so to speak) between himself and Esau by sending ahead huge droves of gift-cattle at spaced intervals. Such gifts would not lack motivation; Jacob is worried about the reception he will get, and he acts toward his brother as man acts toward God. Jacob seeks to appease Esau as Abimelech seeks to appease Sarah for having placed her in compromising circumstances by offering her a monetary gift (20:16). The difference is that Abimelech uses an ordinary, secular expression—*kĕsût ʿênayim* (covering of the eyes)—while Jacob's term is the ordinarily theological term *kippurîm* (atonement understood as the "covering" or overlooking of sin). Jacob calls each gift-drove a *minḥâ*, from the root *mnḥ*, a gift, but suggestive in particular of a sacrificial gift to God—especially if one thinks of a gift going before or mediating for the worshiper (32:21) and the desired effect as "lifting the countenance." Although the Priestly blessing of Numbers 6:26 appeals to God to lift *his* countenance, Jacob's wish is rather extra- than antidevotional; to "raise Jacob's countenance" would be, in ordinary idiom, to accept him, but also to raise him to the level of Esau's regard. What seems so Eisaacic about all this is the suggestion of gracious decorum rather than fear. Piety, civility, righteousness are presented together with a suggestion of pathos—of how moving it is that Jacob so worries about being accepted.

Jacob the writer gives Father Jacob something more to worry about—

and something less ethereal in the atmosphere of mediation. We can represent the difference by supposing that *mal'ākîm* in verse 2 denotes angels (to Eisaac) but suggests (to Jacob the revisionist) the need for earthly messengers. Father Jacob sends messengers to say, "Thus says your servant Jacob: 'I have been dwelling with Laban and been delayed till now'" (32:5). Perhaps this strangely brief greeting is intended only partly as a gesture of grace (phoning ahead) and partly as bark from one who cannot bite: "I have been trailing for a while, preoccupied with other things, but now I have come to claim the priority of place and blessing I previously wrested from you." Like the ram caught in the thicket after the release of Isaac, Jacob-come-lately is *'āḥar* in the sense of having been Number Two, an understudy detained in the wings by the Director until his time was ripe.

But the best-laid Jacobic plans "gang aft agley," and the messengers return with their message undelivered. Esau was already on his way, his physical prevenience preventing Jacob's verbal prevenience. Now a brother's frown seems less the cause than a symbol of the more immediate object of dread: four hundred fast-moving, sword-swinging vigilantes. If it is correct to interpret the whole messengers' passage as Jacobic addition, the sound of those approaching warmongers would drown out the sound of any gift-droves' conciliatory stampede. That is, vivid Jacobic imagination renders pale and ineffectual by contrast the more delicate passage about the gift-droves. Another way: It took only an Eisaacic suggestion about heavenly messengers to conceive of a passage about earthly messengers, and the more terrifying thought of the messengers' defeated purpose heightens the tension beyond its Eisaacic level.

Whether or not these speculations about the origin of the "messengers passage" are vain, there is ample philological and thematic reason to suppose that the passage which follows had no Eisaacic pre-text. Eisaac's conciliatory plan is the set of offerings, the *minḥôt,* while Jacob the revisionist proposes the set of camps, the *maḥănôt.* Besides the Jacobic habits of phrase and the appeal, in prayer, to other Jacobic passages, the new stratagem seems a peculiarly Jacobic misreading of the heavenly vision: Jacob sees not a heavenly host fighting for him, assuring him of divine protection, but a double camp that gives him the idea of dividing his camp in two. If we thus suppose the divided earthly camp to be a play on the heavenly camp, the dual *maḥănayim,* we must be struck by how secular, how antithetical to the Eisaacic is this strategy. But it is not just Jacob's family and possessions that are split in two; his personality is also split, revealing both the practical realist and the Chosen Son, in touch with Yava. The immediate effect is the rather touching figure of one who acknowledges all his success to be God's doing: "I crossed this Jordan with [just] my staff, and now I have become two camps!"

One might call it an irony that the boast "I am two camps!" should conclude a passage of humility and appeal for divine assistance, but "irony" is really the wrong trope. Both Jacobs are engaged, rather, in what Harold Bloom might call the revisionary ratio of *kenosis,* reduction and isolation of the self. Eisaac's Jacob soliloquizes that in being reduced to covering Esau's face (a dead metaphor for atonement), he will be able to face Esau and have his own downcast face uplifted (a metonymy for genial greeting). Jacob's Jacob engages in more radical reduction, isolating himself not only from the gift-droves but from the self-portrait as Jacob-grown-fat. He regresses not just to the stage of eastward-bound wanderer, staff in hand, but back to the childhood wrestling with and wresting from his brother. Sending ahead not just the gift-droves but his entire family, so that he remains alone, the last to cross the Jabbok, Jacob undoes and isolates himself in a regression one might call back to the womb, back to the prenatal wrestling of the twins in Rebecca's womb.

To this limiting *kenosis,* Jacob the revisionist responds with an extraordinary *daemonization*—a demon-making, or putting on the power. Now it is not the dreaded four hundred *'îš* ("men," or *'îš milḥāmâ,* "warriors") but one *'îš,* one dread adversary whose power is "confronted"—and transferred.

Who is this *'îš*? What is his relation to Esau, to the Esau-preferring Isaac, to Isaac's god *paḥad* (Fear), to the hidden face but manifest power of Eisaac, master of the specially delayed and highly charged face-to-face encounter? However we represent the *'îš,* even if we simply say that *'îš* means "man" as trope for "angel, one of the errant members of the heavenly host," we must confront the *'îš* as representation. We must confront, that is, the narrative fact that the daemonization (in the sense of empowering) of Jacob takes place through the daemonization (in the sense of representing-as-demon) of some "other." Toward an understanding of this representation, two avenues of approach deserve special consideration.

We may regard the *'îš* as a demon-emanation from Esau, going out before him, as Jacob's droves and camps go out before him, thus preparing the stage for the half-sublime, half-grotesque nocturnal wrestling match. Like Shakespeare's Orlando in *As You Like It,* Jacob does not wrestle with his older brother directly because a bout with his *'îš,* this old-school, old-reputation "Charles, wrestler to Frederick" substitutes for and prevents the more open representation of brotherly hostility. The identity of the brother-as-other is not so much repressed as re-presented, and a happier resolution is prepared.

If we regard the *'îš* as a figure independent of Esau and related more directly to divine power, we are led to wonder whether something so quintessentially Jacobic as a wrestling match with a god necessarily implies a closer connection between the *'îš* and Yava rather than the Eisaacic deity, who "wouldn't be caught dead"—or defeated—in such circumstances. Although there is hardly a critic who proposes that the nocturnal wrestling match is an E text, the very important pseudoetymology of *Israel* as "striver with El" suggests that strife with this *'îš* may represent Jacobic strife with the Eisaacic El and the text over which he presides. From the perspective of Jacob the revisionist, the normative etymology of *Israel* as "El will fight [on the side of this chosen people]" is all too Eisaacic, too normative a nationalistic sentiment. Perhaps no single misreading could so embody the revisionary theology of Jacob as the redefinition of Israel through the story of the wrestling with an *'îš* who is a messenger, a representative, an angel, or a trope for *El.* Father Jacob and the Children of Jacob will constitute their worthiness by identifying themselves as strivers with the old Eisaacic god, not strivers, with "God on their side," against others.

In proposing that the *'îš* be regarded as a representation of the Eisaacic god El, I wish not merely to add one more name to the roster of identifications previously proposed but to call attention to the Jacobic power of representation—of re-presenting a given power in the old story, or the old theology, in more awe-inspiring and inspired terms. The *'îš* may be Esau's personal guardian angel, the defeat of whom enables the pacific meeting that follows; he may be imagined to be the *genius loci* of Canaan, the spirit whose blessing re-presents to Jacob the blessing previously wrested by a different kind of force, and granting a more authentic "passport" to the returning Possessor of the Land. The *'îš* may be the obedient (or the AWOL) angel of El, agent of the transfer of the kind of benignant power that subdues the dissident and quiets the discontent. He may be regarded as the daemonized form of the abstraction "I am with you" of Gen. 28:15. He may even be regarded as a dark double or doppelgänger, an angel of death—though I should want to add to that identification of Harold Bloom's the specification "angel of Eisaacic death," in the spirit of Keats's wrestling with Milton: "Life to him would be death to me." He might even be called an Arnoldian "righting" of the Miltonic personification of Sin and Death: the *'îš* would allegorically represent the God-idea, the "Power that makes for Righteousness," the wrestling with which "rights" the Jacobic trickster's machinations and the Israelite's strife with his neighbors. "Why do you ask my name?" the *'îš* himself asks. To give one name to the *'îš* may be to limit the power of one of the most powerful Jacobic creations, a creation synechdochally representative of the power of Jacob the revisionist to rename, to refigure, to reopen spaces in the ur-text.

To read the passages about Jacob's disposition of his camp is to confront a character who seems as nervous in revising his plan of action as Jacob the writer is eager to rework the ground of his ur-text. My own view is that the Eisaacic passage in which Jacob sends the gift-droves ahead once ended with "Jacob encamped for the night there" (32:22) and continued with the scene the next morning, a scene filled with sunlight (now in verse 32) and the happy arrival of a benignant brother. The entire detailing of the night's procedures may belong to a single, Jacobic addition:

> He rose that night and took his two wives and two concubines and his eleven children and crossed the Jabbok Ford with them. He [personally] escorted them and took across all that was his. [Crossing back after the last of his camp had traversed the ford,] Jacob remained alone. . . .

There is no reason why the second sentence has to represent an alternate account, something inserted from another documentary source; it reads like nervous elaboration, revisionist Jacob going over the same narrative ground as Father Jacob paces back and forth. From verse 22 through 24 we have five forms of the verb *ʿbr,* the root of *ʿibrî,* a "Hebrew," one who "crosses over." While crossing and recrossing the Jabbok, Jacob is also "going over" the ground previously Abraham's—and reconstituting himself as Hebrew, indeed as *the* Hebrew, coming now to reclaim the promised land. By the time of Deuteronomy, which includes a personal confession to be recited by the Hebrew in recognition of the blessings associated with true settling of the land, Jacob has totally supplanted Abraham as patriarch: "A wandering Aramean was my father," the confession begins (Deut. 26:5)—summarizing essential Hebrew history *from Jacob.* Whether or not there ever was a Jacob cult separate from the worship of the God of Abraham and Isaac, the story as we have it concerns a Jacob who wins his place in line, third of the fathers, but in more than the literal sense *the* father of the Children of Israel.

Before the nocturnal wrestling match, Jacob's thought is to appear last, to come behind his gifts in a posture that suggests renewed humility and secondariness vis-à-vis Esau. The wrestling itself, however, suggests a reevaluation of secondariness. Though Jacob "wins" the match, there can be no greater reward than for the winner to humble himself before the "loser" and receive blessing from him. In this sense, the meaning of the confrontation with the *ʾîš* transcends the reevaluation of Father Jacob's relation to Esau and carries into the realm of the symbolic sublime the figuration of the relation between Jacob the midrashist and his Eisaacic original. The simple truth at the heart of Jacobic narrative is that all blessedness, all inspiration, depends on belatedness, on a strong swerve from a recognized, older line. A river crossing is but a river crossing, a meeting of brothers but a "hail, fellow, well met" where there is no prior investment in the space or relationship that is now being "redistricted." The rabbi who noted that the root of the word for wrestle is the word *'bq*, "dust," grounded in etymology a metaphysics of re-creation: the being who wrestles with Jacob re-creates him, not as first man, from the dust, but as new-first-man, reborn from the earth into a supernaturally sanctioned status, a revisionary "Number One." But perhaps the philological insight of Rashi is yet more acute: if *'bq* (to join) is the Aramaic equivalent of *ḥbq* (to embrace), then the being who "wrestles" (*yē'ābēq*) with Jacob in 32:26 is anticipating the embrace of Esau in 33:4 (*yĕḥabbĕqēhû*). The story of Esau embracing Jacob is one of the great triumphs of Eisaacic imagination, a passage of unusually heightened pathos, humanity, and religious dignity. But the story of Jacob wrestling with the *'îš* is not only one of the great triumphs of Jacobic imagination; it is a story *about* the triumph of Jacobic imagination—of blessing, or inspiration, wrested from a source, and resting now in a source—in the voice of the Jacobic shuttle weaving in and out of the text of Eisaacic warp.

Although I cannot explain why these narratives should bear some philological marks of being retold by Jacob—why even what I regard as the Eisaacic meeting of the brothers in 33:1–17 seems to have undergone some Jacobic rewriting—some of the verbal peculiarities, especially those surrounding the use of divine names, make startling sense. It is God—that is El, Eisaac's god—with whom Jacob the character wrestles in this scene and with whom Jacob the writer wrestles in creating this, and perhaps every major scene. But if *'îš* can be too easily read as a word for angel, we are made to confront *'îš* also as human form, as the fraility, the faultiness, the earthly origins of all that is Eisaacic, which Jacob confronts and reinterprets into the muscular victory of the Human Form Divine. Whether or not we also associate the *'îš* with the "guardian angel" of Esau, the *'îš* who must flee before the dawn is not just any ministering angel but the angel of death, the covering cherub blocking the way of Hebraizing or threshold-crossing Jacob. For Jacob the writer, at least, the *'îš* is the incarnate form of everything that is dead, that is imaginative death, in the tradition. From Jacob's point of view, to be an Israelite is not to be an orthodox jingoist who believes God is on his side, regardless of whether those on the other side are Edomites, Hittites, or modern-day Arabs; to be an Israelite is to wrestle with (in the sense of against) Eisaac's god, to struggle and embrace until the ghastly turns "ghostly"—in the sense of a more authentic spiritual presence. Such wrestling constitutes the true passing on of the blessing, and those who note that Jacob previously usurps what he now receives by divine sanction are entirely correct: The scene prepares for the meeting of Esau and Jacob by rewriting Jacob's spiritual portfolio in the nick of time. It is a portfolio signed and sealed not by Jacob's Yava (not by Yava so named) but by Eisaac's Elohim, whom Jacob's Jacob has seen—as metaphor becomes myth—face to face.

If the meaning of the wrestling scene is a function of intertextuality, the impression left by the scene itself, at least in a naïve reading, is of a Jacobic flair above and beyond the quarrels for priority and place. This flair comes from a dramatic human action so different, so strongly foregrounded against the intertextual or intertheological conflicts. Background falls away—or rather, setting, literal setting, becomes part of the dramatic action. In the beautiful sentence concluding the wrestling scene, the sun becomes an actor previously sighted but now in full-stage: "As he passed over Penuel, the sun rose upon him" (32:32). This normative expression may lose some of the force of the literal meaning of *wayyizraḥ-lô haššemeš*—the sun rose for him. Whatever the metaphysical or physical threat of the nocturnal spirit who flees with the dawn, the night has passed and the bell has not tolled for Jacob. Ask not the name of the *'îš*, nor for whom the sun shines: it shines for thee!

To feel that the sun shines for you is to feel the Jacobic equivalent of what Eisaac would call the beneficence of God shining his countenance upon thee and being gracious unto thee. The special savor of the Jacobic blessing is the lack of distance between its metaphysical component and its physical representation. This sunrise savors of the same blessing that Jacob's Jacob receives in 27:27: "The smell of my son is like the smell of a field Yava has blessed." In the Eisaacic scene of reunion between Jacob and Esau, the sweet savor comes rather from the sunshine of human joy. Wonder to behold, it takes no preliminary words at all for the brothers to be drawn together. Esau runs to greet Jacob, embraces him, kisses him, weeps over him. For all Jacob's anxiety about Esau and the possible threat posed by his four hundred men, Esau's greeting is totally "disarming." It takes only this silent moment to put far off the thought of power struggle between brothers or writers. And yet, magnificent as the moment is, the climax of the scene is not in the silence but in an extraordinary Eisaacic remark. Esau inquires about the sublime excess of the gifts Jacob has sent, and Jacob explains first in terms of a previous intention and then—miraculously—in terms of a presently revised motive: "It was to find favor in your eyes—so please, take the gift from my hands because seeing your face is like seeing the face of God—and you have been gracious unto me" (33:10). The gift changes from a peace offering to a thanksgiving offering without losing its aspect of *minḥâ,* of sacrificial offering to God. The supreme, Eisaacic sublimity of this moment may be summarized in what Shakespeare's Bassanio confronts as the necessity of "hazarding all he has": throwing God himself into metaphor, into the *as if* that serves a human end. We cannot call this extraordinary moment an allusion to the previous night's encounter, the "reality" that this meeting is "like." Precisely the contrary; it is the force of this extraordinary Eisaacic moment that appears now to be the origin of the Jacobic encounter invented to prevent it—to go before and overpower it.

Like Esau, the reader may feel pressed upon by verse 11 to accept the offering of Jacob: "Take my blessing that I have brought you because God has been gracious to me and because I have everything." The previous verse's *minḥa* (offering) becomes *bĕrākâ* (blessing) as Eisaacic text transcends the limits ordinarily distinguishing it from Jacobic revision. Just as it is hard for people to accept gifts when the kindness seems excessive to the point of infringement, so the excess greatness of the Eisaacic passage may pose a particular difficulty for Jacob the revisionist. It is a difficulty confronted when Jacob's return of the "blessing" to Esau is matched by the receipt of the new blessing from the *'îš*.

If the vision of Esau meeting Jacob face to face seems to carry with it the vision of a transcendence of time in which Eisaac could confront Jacob, both sublimities collapse before the realities of history. The brothers do not live together, any more than Eisaac and Jacob could occupy the same space. Henceforth, as Jacob says to Esau in regard to their literal wanderings, "I will follow at a slower pace" (33:14). As we turn from the stories of Jacob in his own generation to those of Dinah and Joseph, Jacob's children, we turn away from the dramatic face-to-face. A dim sight of divine providence takes over where divine presence was seen before, and the blind work of human hands becomes more and more problematic.

Holy War

> In a little community like ours, my dear . . . we have a general number one. That is, you can't consider yourself as number one without considering me too as the same and all the other young people.
>
> —Fagan in *Oliver Twist*

Although the Eisaacic and Jacobic stories of Dinah are both tales of crusade against the heathen, the stories differ enough from each other to invite us to regard the Jacobic version as waging a war of its own against the Eisaacic story and the Eisaacic values for which it stands. The Eisaacic story is a story not about rape but about the threat of assimilation. Its violence is not without pathos—the pathos that comes from a knowing sacrifice of something noble but pagan, something that may be admired but must be dismissed before the greater claims of the God of Israel. Here is the Eisaacic story:

> Dinah, the daughter of Leah whom she bore to Jacob, went out to call upon the girls native to the place. Shechem, son of Hamor the Hivite, prince of the land, saw her and liked the lass. Shechem spoke to Hamor his father, requesting, "Get me that girl for a wife."
>
> Hamor, father of Shechem, went forth to speak to Jacob. The sons of Jacob heard of this and came from the field. And so Hamor spoke to them all: "Shechem, my son, has his heart set on your daughter. Would you folks be so kind as to give her to him for a wife? Let us intermarry: Give us your daughters and take our daughters for your own. Dwell with us and the land will lie before you to dwell in, to trade in, to hold as possession."
>
> Shechem then spoke up, addressing [Dinah's] father and brothers: "Let me find favor in your eyes! Whatever you ask of me, I will give. Ask of me ever so much dowry and portion, I will give it as you demand it of me; only give me the girl for a wife."
>
> The sons of Jacob answered Shechem and Hamor, his father, guilefully. They said, "We would not be able to do this thing—to give our sister to an uncircumcised man, for it is a shameful thing to us. Only on this condition could we accommodate you: if you would be like us, circumcising every male. Then we would give our daughters to you and take your sons for our own and dwell with you and be one people. But if you do not heed us on the matter of circumcision, we will take our daughter and be off."
>
> Their words pleased Hamor and Shechem. Hamor and Shechem came to the gate of their city and spoke with the people of their city, saying: "These people are peacefully inclined toward us; they would dwell in the land, develop trade, and the land will be broad enough to accommodate them; we will take their daughters for wives, and we will give them our daughters. Only on one condition will the people agree to dwell with us to be one people: we must circumcise every male as they are circumcised. Shall not their cattle, their possessions, and all their animals be ours? Only let us be agreeable to them and they will dwell with us!" All the adults of the city listened to Hammor and Shechem; all the adults were circumcised.
>
> On the third day, while they were in pain, the sons of Jacob each took his sword and marched brazenly on the city. They slew all the males; they spoiled the city and took the sheep, cattle, asses, and everything that was in the city or in the field: all their wealth, all their children and wives they took captive; they took for spoil everything in the home. (From chapter 34)

This is not a primitive story, although it describes some action we may judge morally primitive. Because God is not a speaker or actor in the tale, we may regard it as a forerunner of the providential story fully developed in regard to Joseph. Yet the Joseph story "experiments" with God's absence only to assure us, in the end, of the Divine Hand operating behind the scene of history. This Eisaacic story of Dinah comes round to no such assurance. It is a story about how men take it upon themselves to fight God's cause, and it is written from a bittersweet consciousness of being "in the right." If we can characterize as "primitive" the story of the Good defeating the Evil, we can see why such a tale, so far from seeming innocent and untouchable, would have posed a particular threat, or at least a particularly alluring possibility for revision, to Jacob.

Eisaac's story may be said to lure Jacob as the reader of Eisaac's story is lured to sympathy with Shechem and Hamor. It is possible that Hamor's name is itself the product of Jacobic revision, for *ḥămôr* means "ass," and it will be Jacob's effort to portray this father as too willing to make an ass of himself. But in the Eisaacic story, the relation between Hivite father and son is full of dignity. Shechem is attracted to Dinah, and he asks his father to procure the girl in marriage. His father understands that what is involved is no one-time intermarriage but a question of the cultural future of his people and Jacob's. He comes to Jacob with a proposal for peaceful coexistence. To a nationalistic ear, this cry of "Peace!" is no peace but the threat of assimilation, and something of this belated perspective is represented in the story when Hamor and Shechem explain to the elders of their city that intermarriage will mean what is Jacob's will be theirs, not vice versa. Yet there is something appealing about those Hivites, and it is the age-old appeal of the Old Money to the newcomers on the make. The Hivites have manners on their side, and they couple such grace with a sweet reasonableness that looks like a more sophisticated version of revelation. Eisaac may wish us to regard God alone as the proper dispenser of the land, but Eisaac is willing to portray the lure of a wholly secular parallel to the promise God made to Abraham: "Dwell with us; the earth is all before you! Make yourselves at home; develop commerce; gain possession; become the Establishment." Shechem's good breeding and political caution, exemplified by subordinating himself to his father as ambassador, contrasts painfully with the vulgarity of the sons of Jacob, who supplant their father and enter the dialogue like brutes: "If you have something to say to Jacob, speak to us." Hamor tacitly acknowledges that the Children of Israel "are" Israel, and he addresses them as though Dinah were daughter of the assembled collectivity. It is the sons of Jacob who are specifically described as proceeding *bĕmirmâ,* "with guile." We may wish to specify that the most sophisticated "guile" belongs to Eisaac, the author who portrays as a genuine sacrifice and no slaughter the sacrifice of gentility before the God Who Brooks Not the Gentiles.

An unusual play on words may represent, in miniature, the sophistication of this Eisaacic story and its vulnerability to Jacobic assault. The sons of Jacob lay before Hamor and Shechem one condition: *'ak-bĕzō't nē'ôt lākem* ("Only with this will we consent to you," 34:15, and forms of this rare verb are repeated in 22 and 23). Coming from the root *'wt,* the verb *nē'ôt* may suggest giving pleasure, and thus oneself consenting. But the same three letters of the root spell the noun *'ôt* (sign, symbol, testimonial), a word that was crucial to the covenant of circumcision in 17:11, and a word on which the claims and counterclaims of secular adaptation may be said to hinge. In making the covenant with Abraham, the Eisaacic God leaves somewhat ambiguous whether the human obligation is to "walk before [God] and be pure" (17:1) or whether circumcision itself is the man's half of the bargain. We may regard this ambiguity as central to Judaism, or at least central to Eisaacic religion. But in the offer that the sons of Jacob make to the Hivites, circumcision is no sign representing something else—the acceptance of the yoke of religious responsibility. It is an empty signifier that, if accepted as such, would indeed guarantee the assimilation of the two peoples into one. The lure to the Hivites is the lure of dismissing religious differences as empty signs. If the story thus allegorizes assimilation, the bloody end of the Hivites represents a pathetic but necessary rebloodying of an abstraction. Like the *'ăqēdâ,* the Eisaacic Dinah story pushes the believer to the brink of disgust with the arbitrariness and power of the God to be worshiped; but like the *'ăqēdâ* story again, the Eisaacic Dinah story is intended to return its audience to more profound allegiance.

Let us turn to the Jacobic transformation of the Dinah story by considering the model of the Canterbury pilgrims whose stories seem to arise out of their interaction. In Chaucer, the word *quite* can express either an appropriate match ("somewhat to quite with the Knightes tale") or the mode of "requital" ("ful wel coude I thee quite," says the Reeve to the Miller) that has more to do with revenge than with an abstract sense of suitability in kind. In Genesis, the root *šlm* can be associated with a similar duality. We think of the root most commonly in the form of *šālôm* (peace, security), but it can also refer to the kind of payment in full that denotes total destruction or "total return" in the sense of "requital." Buried in Eisaac's story of Dinah is an explosively ironic use of this root. Shechem and Hamor report of the sons of Jacob, *hā'ănāšîm ha'ēlleh šĕlēmîm hēm 'ittānû,* "these people are at peace with us" (34:21). Ostensibly, these children of Jacob are at peace; they have bought the land they occupy from Hamor, and they appear to be amenable to intermarriage and assimilation. Yet it is Eisaac's intention to show that the Children of Israel cannot be at peace with their neighbors if that peace is a wholly secular establishment, a covenant between nations that replaces the covenant with God. When Abraham first arrives at Shechem (12:6), he receives a promise of the land, a promise that it seems must brook some delay: "In the fourth generation they shall come here again; for the iniquity of the Amorite is not yet full" (15:16). The Hebrew uses the word *šālēm* to denote that missing fullness. In this dignified, if peculiar, notion of divine justice, dispossession is based on loss of moral virtue. Perhaps Jacob interprets the old Eisaacic promise to refer to possession of Canaanite land after Isaac (second generation), Jacob (third), and Jacob's children (fourth) will have found reason to measure the fullness of the iniquity of the local inhabitants. But whether or not it is plausible that Jacob responds to an inner moral imperative to weigh the native population and find it wanting, we may consider the possibility that he responds to a literary imperative to make whole (to make into a shaped, literary whole) a story of no peace. Jacob appears to signal his attention to the ironies of *šālēm* (completed) and *šĕlēmîm* (at peace) by describing Jacob the character arriving *šālēm* (33:18)—not to the city of Shalem, as has been supposed, but "at peace," with an (ironically premature) sense of resolution of conflict with outsiders over possession of the land.

I wish, then, to propose that Jacob undermines the gentle pathos of Eisaac's story of Dinah by substituting for its decorous assessment of the dangers of assimilation a less decorous but more shockingly *šālēm* (whole, complete, "paid up") story of iniquity and punishment. Like the Eisaacic story of the purchase of Sarah's burial place from Ephron the Hittite (23:3–20), the Eisaacic story of the purchase of Jacob's dwelling place (33:19–20) smooths over the difficulties about conquest of the land by offering a "paid up" account in the most civilized mode of such transactions—money. Jacob, however, deals not in civilities but in the more passionate medium of moral right and wrong—or rather, in the medium of fiery passion to which charges of moral right and wrong serve as fuel. It is the iniquity of the Amorites that has to be "paid up," rendered *šālēm,* or complete, before the fourth generation from Abraham can possess the land (15:16), and it is the iniquity of the Hivites in chapter 34 that Jacob sets out to detail. The violence of Jacob the writer on the Eisaacic text is the violence of Shechem on Dinah, for *in the Jacobic version, Shechem does not simply desire her but rapes her.* "He took her, he lay with her, he afflicted her." A peculiarity of the Masoretic text alerts us to the sort of aggression that language can perform as well as describe. The Masoretic text reads *wayyiškab ʾōtāh,* he "laid her," with the vulgar accusative, as opposed to *wayyiškab ʾittāh,* he "lay with her." Whether such a change crept into the text early or late, we can label it "Jacobic." The same might be said for Shechem's request to his father, which changes *naʿărā* (damsel, maid) to *yaldâ* (girl): The effect is to diminish the graciousness of Shechem's deference to his father by substituting the boorishness of the colloquial "Get me that girl!"

Insofar as the composition of Genesis is literary composition, not a redactor's distillate of social attitudes and political allegiances, Jacob's quarrel is with Eisaac rather than with the Hivites as such. Jacob mocks the Eisaacic morality with a sentence less pious than what is colloquially called "wicked": "The sons of Jacob came from the field when they heard, and the men were sad; they were very angry because a terrible thing was done in Israel: To lay the daughter of Jacob—this is not to be done!" This is ostensibly Eisaacic in sentiment, but clearly not of Eisaacic composition. One might argue that since Dinah is, at this point, the only "Israelite" girl, there is no need to specify a law prohibiting extramarital relations with the daughters of Israel in general. Yet the effect of the singular "daughter of Israel" is compounded by the coupling of the phrase with *wĕkēn lōʾ yēʿāśeh* ("that's not to be done," or "that's not the way we do things around here!"). If vigilante justice is replacing sweet, negotiable reason, we will not be surprised to find that Jacob imagines Dinah to have remained in Shechem's possession while negotiations proceed. In Jacob's version, Dinah has to be brought back by force, rescued from the enemy camp. What is surprising is the directness with which Jacob assaults the Eisaacic text at its priestly core. In place of "the sons of Jacob took each man his sword," Jacob inserts the specification, "two of the sons of Jacob, Simeon and Levi, Dinah's brothers, took each man his sword, and confidently marched on the city, slaying every male" (34:25). Now Jacob the writer had a number of sons of Jacob to choose from, assuming that he wished to single out two of the brothers. Why not Reuben, Judah, Issachar, Zebulun? By singling out Levi, Jacob attacks the entire priestly establishment of Eisaacic religion: The Levites have no portion in the land of Israel not because they are holier but because they are more brutal than the rest. Simeon is a tribe whose land allotment as enclaves within Judah likewise indicates a punishment rather than a special merit. The coupling of Levi and Simeon thus becomes a nastiness of its own. Yet should anyone complain that the priestly account is not fully "paid up," at peace with poetic justice, Jacob might retort that the slaying of three thousand fellow Israelites in Exodus 32 accounts for the choice of Levi alone. The story of Dinah but prepares the way for that supreme nastiness, the choice of the house of Levi because of its bloodthirsty zeal.

One final set of Jacobic "fingerprints" can be read from the tale as it has been left to us. Father Jacob complains that Simeon and Levi have troubled him, that they have put him in an embarrassing position in relation to other inhabitants of the land (*lĕhabʾîšēnî*, "to embarrass"). Like Eisaac, Father Jacob may be deeply concerned with the survival of the race, a survival that was threatened by assimilation at first and now by hostile attack. Yet the Jacob who worries about the impression he is making seems an incorrigibly "civil" forefather. The people called the "children of Israel" really derive from the spirit of Jacob's literal children, the spirit of righteous indignation ready to blot out the decorum of the written, Eisaacic account, and ready to blot out the lives of the old inhabitants of the land where they stand in the way. Genesis ends with a subtler meditation on the Eisaacic sense of providence; but we turn to the story of Joseph and its delicate triumph over fraternal hostility having seen what internecine aggression can be.

·6·

JOSEPH'S INCREASE

> These patients regularly repeat the traumatic situation in their dreams. . . . The term "traumatic" has no other sense than an economic one. We apply it to an experience which within a short period of time presents the mind with an increase of stimulus too powerful to be dealt with or worked off in the normal way.
>
> —Freud, *General Theory of the Neuroses*

Any literary interpreter of the concluding chapters of Genesis must contemplate the pace of the story in discussing its meanings. Why should it take several elegant chapters to get Jacob and his family down to Egypt when it took only a few, confused verses to get Abraham to Canaan? Whether we think of a narrative as fast or slow depends on whether we regard events along the way as components of a single line of family history, or whether an array of events seems a form of elaboration, a way of lingering over essential relationships and themes. The story of Joseph is *a* story, a leisurely story, in just this sense that its episodes have the quality of variations on a theme: its several reversals in the order of family privilege seem like meditations on the concept of natural vs. antithetical or divinely sanctioned order; the many descents to Egypt seem to be lingering over the theme of descent rather than simply hastening through accounts of several distinct journeys.

Because the slowed pace seems tied to a sense of an ending, it is difficult to regard the division of Genesis from the remainder of the Pentateuch as a belated and arbitrary deed. The question of pace becomes part of the "content" of the story, especially when Joseph protracts the revelation of his identity to his brothers and then immediately shifts the focus from his plans to the divine, providential plan for the well-being of the family: "And now be not grieved . . . for God sent me before you to preserve life" (45:5). He seems to be summing up a perspective toward which the whole book—at least the Eisaacic book—has been aiming. Even this revelatory sentence may have been "slowed" by revisionary addition, although there may be some question whether the words of consolation or the specification that the brothers sold Joseph is the Jacobic contribution. But in considering pace as a key to the composition of the story, we might do well to linger, in a preliminary way, on the concept of midrash as leisurely expansion.

The study of literature suggests two models for the understanding of a slowed narrative pace. For one, we may recur to Dr. Johnson's complaint that "Where there is leisure for fiction there is little room for grief." Now leisure for fiction *is* the elegiac mode, and the entire Joseph story may be regarded as an elegy for Jacob. It begins with 37:2, "These are the generations of Jacob," and runs through the impressive funeral and mourning for Jacob, marked by a redescent to Egypt, a renewed reconciliation of the brothers, and perhaps even by the death of Joseph as the last reflection or repetition in a finer (less stentorious) tone of the theme of the close of the patriarchal period.

The elegiac mode remains, *pace* Dr. Johnson, quintessentially leisurely—and Eisaacic. Beside it, we may put a second general category of thought about leisure that may be described as less tempered or plaintive, however poignant. Here leisure is the concomitant of self-absorption, not anxiety, because a sense of mastery—of surety about an approaching consummation of a narrative, like a sexual act—prompts a relaxation of the pace. Instead of fretting about Jacob the character we glory in the most extended display of the prowess of Jacob the narrator. For although the books of Exodus and Numbers contain much of what documentary scholars call "J" material, I do not think we can regard these works as having anything like the coherent Jacobic perspective that I have been arguing for in Genesis. Exodus and Numbers sparkle here and there with J moments, but the hypothesis of a written document, reinterpreted and expanded by a brilliant Jacobic revisionist, would necessarily entail, after Genesis, something closer to the usual "fragmentary hypothesis." "R" becomes more distant from "J." Whatever the revisionist motives for variation in Exodus, there is a remarkable increase in the amount of extraliterary, partisan tinkering once we get to Mosaic revelation.

In Jacobic fiction-making, distraction is not tolerated out of ostensible weakness but invited as a privilege of strength. Wordsworth beautifully describes the coming-on of this leisure for fiction in the poem "Nutting," when the narrator finds just the scene he has been looking for, ripe and ready for him:

> A little while I stood,
> Breathing with such suppression of the heart
> As joy delights in; and, with wise restraint
> Voluptuous, fearless of a rival, eyed
> The banquet.

One might call "midrashic" Wordsworth's turn from the scene before him to the scene not there. Indeed, he goes on not just to imagine a rich, faeryland landscape complete with "water breaks" that "murmur on forever," but to declare, with something like prophetic strain, "and I saw the sparkling foam." While this notion of the visionary may be especially interesting to a reading of Jacobic epiphany, I quote the poem here because of what it specifies as the sense of triumph, of joy "fearless of a rival." For in turning to the Joseph saga we turn, I believe, to two rival notions of the leisure for fiction—the Eisaacic, elegiac notion of a consummation *devoutly* to be wished, and the Jacobic, imaginative victory "fearless of a rival," that is (reading behind or against such denial), the rival-*conscious* theory of composition in which a victory over death is a victory over and against a precursor. Perhaps it is no accident that Wordsworth's poem ends by turning from the Jacobic to the Eisaacic with the perception of a "spirit in the woods," for the sublimation of sexual mastery into spiritual presence is at the core of Wordsworth's sometimes brilliantly controlled, sometimes unconscious returns to Eisaacic piety—to what we might call Eisaacic "narrative theory" or invention *as* religiosity. The Jacobic narrative strain, on the other hand, achieves startling originality precisely through its awareness of struggle: The agon with what I have taken to be a precursor text is an agon with death, and hence so many of the Jacobic stories end with reassurance about continuity of the generations, rather than continuity of "spirit" manifest as transcendent being.

The Eisaacic Joseph narrative discovers "a spirit in the woods," a spirit called Elohim but experienced, without face-to-face confrontation, as the nameless presence, Divine Providence. If it makes any sense to single out a particular psychological mechanism of defense as characteristic of a narrator, we might think of Eisaacic sublimation as both the general bias toward spiritual themes and the particular orientation of the Genesis narrative as a whole toward the vaporization of the idea of divinity into the purer essence of providence at work behind, rather than in the foreground of, history. Although God is much discussed in the Eisaacic story, he does not appear until 46:2, even in dreams. His presence is sensed in the phenomenon of significant dreams, and his power is manifest as the power to interpret dreams. It takes narrative time, not apocalypse, for him to be felt.

The Interpretation of Seams

Our story, our Eisaacic story, begins with dreams—two of them, and the first of three sets of two dreams each. According to the handsome and decorous commentary by Robert Alter on this episode, young Joseph dreams two dreams because the text foretells Joseph's dual role as sovereign and provider in Egypt. In the case of the other two sets, Joseph interprets for us whether the dreams mean the same (for Pharaoh) or differently (for butler and baker). Here, however, the similarity of meaning seems all too evident, annoyingly evident to the brothers. No one is tempted to ask Joseph to interpret these first two dreams, for he has, in repeating them, already spoken too much. There is, throughout the Eisaacic tale, a moral value to silence that is parallel to the religious value of trusting providence and the literary value of subtlety. Everyone has dreams, but only the fool (perhaps the divinely guided fool) broadcasts unwelcome music. As a matter of proper relationship between man and man and between man and God, silence is "guarded" by Jacob: *wĕʾābîw šāmar ʾet-haddābār* (his father "observed" the matter, he "kept it in mind" [37:11]). Were Eisaacic piety unchallenged by Jacobic irony and cultic practice, this quiet mindfulness might have remained the truest form of "observance." The Eisaacic story of Joseph consistently holds such observance as religious ideal, a form of prophetic activity—or rather inactivity, patience—become daily practice.

In the Jacobic revision of the Joseph story, speech—honest, efficacious speech—will challenge Eisaacic silence as a synecdoche for moral value. Indeed, the whole shape of the story may be shifted by the emphasis on power of speech as opposed to silent "observing of the time." It is possible that the specification of hatred for Joseph's dreams *and words about them* is a Jacobic addition, for scholars have long recognized as part of a separate J strand the inability of the brothers to "speak peace" (37:4). In the Jacobic commentary on the essentially Eisaacic story, a spell is cast, as it were, by which the brothers cannot speak to Joseph. Isaac's silent observance becomes not a blessing but a curse, a curse not broken until Joseph's tears release them: "And he kissed all his brothers, and wept over them; after that his brothers [were able to] talk with him" (45:15). Two other details of the initial setting may be attributed to Jacobic rewriting: The coat that is a mark of paternal favoritism Jacob specifies as *kĕtōnet passîm,* a coat with long sleeves, a coat of lordship worn by those chosen people (like academics and clerics) who do not have to work for a living. Second, Jacob's preference for Joseph becomes the prevenient cause of the brothers' hostility. If it is the highest form of Eisaacic narrative piety to sublimate epiphany into providence, it is the essence of Jacobic humanism to reimagine a theological conflict as one between brothers. Jacob the writer cannot "unwrite" the dreams that I am supposing to have been as familiar to his audience as they are to schoolchildren today, but he could add the element of paternal favoritism that precedes and colors the "dreamier" Eisaacic account.

It is interesting to compare the idea of divine intervention, within a story, to the idea of authorial intervention, Eisaacic or Jacobic. In a sense we have been doing this all along, but the Eisaacic Joseph story is so much a story about the sublimation or disappearance of overt intervention that the very idea of revisionist "intervention" has about it something of the antithetical spirit. At one point, Jacob may be inserting a direct revelation absent in his source: The "man" who redirects Joseph from Shechem to Dothan looks like a manifestation of Yava brought in to rewrite and overdetermine the providential sequence of events that follows. (This epiphany may be contrasted to—indeed, it may have been occasioned by—the Eisaacic "resanctioning" of Jacob's descent to Egypt in 46:2–5). Jacobic revision, perhaps even here, works in the direction of undermining the ethereal sense of Eisaacic providence by adding snatches of more human dialogue, more immediate narrative event.

Consider the extraordinary scene as the brothers behold Joseph from afar and plot against him. Idiomatic expression (*ʾîš ʾel-ʾāḥîw* and *baʿal haḥălōmôt*) suggests that their taunt "Look who's coming! If it isn't the master of dreams!" (37:19) is part of an Eisaacic tale. But we cannot be sure about the irony that follows: Let's kill him, throw his body in a ditch, say that a wild animal ate him, "and we'll see what kind of dreams he'll have then!"—or "we'll see what will become of his dreams!" This kind of irony looks like the proleptic irony of the *ʿăqēdâ*, "God will provide a lamb for the altar" (22:8). Indeed, the irony here concerns the same sort of play on what will be naturally or supernaturally revealed. My own guess is that in the *ʿăqēdâ* we have an Eisaacic irony so rich that one may be tempted—wrongly tempted—to suppose it a Jacobic insertion: Abraham thinks that God has provided Isaac, while God has provided, rather, a literal lamb. Here, the brothers similarly believe that they know the thing they speak not—"we'll see what will become of his dreams" means, they think, "that will be the end of his dreams!" The Jacobic-looking twist is that they will see something they do not intend; they will see that his dreams will come to reality. Later, Jacob will say to his sons, "Why do you sit around looking at one another?" (42:1)—where the same verb (or rather, the similar conjugation of the different roots *rʾh*, "sight," and *yrʾ*, "fear") could suggest prophetic insight: Why are you sitting around, trying to "divine" an end to our troubles when there is a course of action you could be taking? And when the returned brothers discover their money in their sacks (42:28), they "look to one another" in fear. Looking at one another displaces the fear they do have and the prophetic insight they do not have in looking at the Joseph they do not recognize. And "fear of Joseph" itself displaces the "fear of God" and the observing of the time, the "looking to divine providence" that are the two faces of Eisaacic piety.

I believe the intricacy and beauty of these connections are essentially

Eisaacic, and that the presence of so developed and overriding a web of ironies constituted one of the major challenges to Jacob. In turning to the particulars of Jacobic revision, we must be wary to acknowledge just how well-wrought a tale was already there. While we must not fall into the trap of saying that the line "we will see what will become of his dreams!" *must* be Jacobic because it is so good, so rich an irony, we must also not fall into the dark pit of obliviousness to the threat that such a sophisticated line poses to a revisionary consciousness. My guess is that both full expression of the brothers' collective plan and the individual, redemptive plan of Reuben are part of the original, Eisaacic text, a text that is then arrested by Jacob for a new and remarkable narrative wrinkle.

Scholars of the documentary hypothesis point to two parallel salvific efforts—those of Reuben and Judah. According to the notion that we have here two separate strands, imperfectly spliced, the action of Judah in forestalling the murder of Joseph is parallel, rather than consequent, to the action of Reuben. Each of them devises a way of coping with the brothers' aggression (perhaps also their own, at least in the case of Judah) while literally shedding no blood. Yet besides the element of alternative, there is also an element of sequence that the "fragmentary hypothesis" does not explain. Reuben's thought is *lō᾽ nakkennû nāpeš*—let us "get him," but not to the point of death; let us give it to him, but not once and for all (37:21). He therefore says, *᾽al tišpĕkû-dām,* "spill no blood," and *yād ᾽al-tišlĕḥû-bô,* "cast no hand against him"—the latter phrase recalling the first intervention of the angel in the *ʿăqēdâ, ᾽al-tišlaḥ yādkā ᾽el-hannʿar,* "cast not your hand against the youth" (22:12). Reuben is thinking of lending a helping hand to Joseph to raise him out of the pit, but what he says depends on a distinction between "killing" and "spilling blood." The appeal of his speech lies in that it seems to allow the brothers to have it both ways, to express their aggression by causing Joseph's death yet escape vengeance—now more specifically associated with the figure of speech, "spilling blood." Reuben at this point conceals his intention to rescue Joseph. But he also conceals from the brothers or buries out of sight the recognition that killing by bloodletting and killing by abandoning the victim to starve to death are both forms of killing.

Judah's plan likewise involves a play on the question of literal or figurative death: To sell Joseph is also to get rid of him, but through a cleaner plan, one with "no hands," neither hands covered with blood-guilt nor hands rescuing Joseph from the pit. Literally, Judah says, "What is the use of killing our brother and covering his blood?" (37:26). Covering, concealing, putting in a pit out of sight will not put guilt out of mind. And so Judah's plan involves openly sharing with the brothers the turn from literal to figurative death: Let us together kill him, *as it were,* and then in place of hidden and revealed meanings, blood shed and blood concealed, we can all face one another. We will even be able to look our father in the face, for we will have no literal death to hide. True enough, we will not be revealing our intention to harm, but what is concealed, we can happily remind ourselves, is the figurative nature of the death. In this "screen memory" version of guilt, one can enjoy the secret knowledge that the hidden fact is not so dark as either appearance or intention.

If it is correct thus to read Judah's plan not as an alternate story of one brother's mediatory intentions but as a revisionary story, then it is probably correct to see the brothers sitting down to eat—while Joseph is in the pit—as part of the revision. That is, the Eisaacic text simply has the brothers throw Joseph in the pit, while Jacob's midrashic addition has them at leisure—eating, observing a passing caravan of Ishmaelites, and listening to Judah's alternate plan to sell Joseph.

A revisionary intention (to sell Joseph rather than slay him) and a revisionary drama of interaction (Judah now the efficacious speaker, the one who commands the others' attention as he will later, in a second Jacobic addition, command Joseph's attention): End of midrashic insertion. We return to the Eisaacic story in which Midianite tradesmen rescue Joseph, only adding the Jacobic insertion that the Midianites sell Joseph to the Ishmaelites, who bring him to Egypt. *The brothers do not sell Joseph.* This last wrinkle looks, perhaps, like an Eisaacic irony at Jacob's expense, since the old story proceeds without the brothers carrying out the sale. Yet I believe the final irony of the recombination is Jacob's, for it belongs to the plot of the reviser that the brothers are left with the foiled intention to sell him; they are left, as it were, still "within" the plot to kill. Stuck in the unrevised plot, they are all the more stuck with the unrevisability of blood guilt. A divine irony—or more properly speaking, a revisionist's extraordinary literary irony—operates to make the foiling of one plan look like a fixation on the previous one. Not only is Judah less kindly than Reuben; the brothers collectively seem more closely associated with the original plan. Reuben's Eisaacic piety is the real loser in the shift, for the lovely simplicity of his intention to restore Joseph to his father now seems all the more like naïveté.

As this first episode draws to a close, Jacob (the character) is left mourning for Joseph and refusing to be comforted. The linguistic evidence points to this being Jacob's Jacob who will not be comforted, but more important than the idea that the words for comfort and underworld are "J" is the rich irony of the phrase *ʾērēd ʾel-bĕnî ʾābel* (I shall descend to my son mourning, 37:35). It will be to the underworld of Egypt that Jacob will descend, and he will mourn until he sees Joseph's face. Jacob's persistence seems all the more moving because of the increase in the vagaries of his children's plots. Jacob's intention to mourn is fixed, and he adheres to this intent with something like, but not too like, Eisaacic piety, the patient "observance" of what God has in store.

Continence and Its Discontents

The story of Joseph's continence in Potiphar's house has about it an element of interlude and an element of added invention. The latter comes from our recognition that the story of Joseph's degradation and ascent would cohere without the Potiphar's wife episode: Joseph could have been simply sold to the prison guard, "master of the executions," where he served as subordinate corrections officer and had occasion to hear and interpret the two dreams of baker and cup-bearer. It may indeed be that the story at one stage cohered without the Potiphar's wife episode, but I believe this would have been not the Eisaacic but a pre-Eisaacic stage. The Potiphar's wife story is itself so much an Eisaacic interlude, in phrasing and in moral outlook, that we must see it as the saga's synecdoche for life itself, for pious living between the Promise and the Revelation. Perhaps these terms suggest Christian homily rather than ancient, ur-Judaic folktale, but it is characteristic of Eisaacic writing that the moral perspective should suggest belated, "improved" vision, however early and original the tale.

If scholars of the documentary hypothesis have consistently labeled the tale a J source, this is because it is framed by material that is undoubtedly J. In 39:1–6 the *bĕrākâ,* the benevolent presence of Yava, descends to Egypt with Joseph, and this sense of assured success overrides—as it might similarly be said to be "written over"—the story of Joseph's integrity. But the core, Eisaacic tale of Potiphar's wife is parallel in outlook to that of Abraham on his way to sacrifice his son: Both are intended to "justify the ways of God to man" by showing us the moral virtue of the hero as just cause for his special selection. The idioms of lifting one's eyes (39:7), as Abraham did (22:13), and of being denied nothing (39:9), as Abraham denied God nothing (22:16), as well as the concept of sinning against God, suggest the Eisaacic hand. So too does the thematic repetition of the garment left behind—now willfully left behind in a gesture that sublimates earlier violence into spirituality. (This is, indeed, the one place where "sublimation" in the original sense of the redirection of *sexual* energy for cultural purposes is relevant.) This Eisaacic tale thus reworks the degradation of Joseph with no hands upon him: Now it is just his integrity—not some character flaw such as garrulousness or spiritual pride—that accounts for his temporary degradation, and now it is just his integrity—not the arbitrary whim of the deity—that accounts for his ultimate rise to glory. This much is the Eisaacic meaning of the story of Potiphar's wife. But all this is then revised by Jacob—preceded and followed by Jacobic assurance about the presence of Yava. Thus, although these verses may seem more crude than the moral fable that they frame, we can understand their presence by viewing them as no alternative statements of providence but revisionary, undermining statements of Yava's interference. It is against Joseph's continence—or more precisely against the Eisaacic use of Joseph's continence to represent the internalization of providence as piety—that Jacob acts to frame the story with a bold assertion of Yava's interference.

Besides these tinkerings, these realignments of given material, the story of Potiphar's wife also impelled a major outburst of antithetical creativity on the part of Jacob: the Tamar story. One way of introducing the Tamar story as midrash is to consider an actual rabbinic midrash on a related matter. In Gen. 24:1 we read that the Lord *bērak ʾet-ʾabrāhām bakkōl* (Yava blessed Abraham in all things), and Rashi explains that the numerical value of *bakkōl* (all things) is the same as *bēn* (son). Since God blessed Abraham with a son (which is as good as being blessed in all things), it was incumbent on Abraham to look to "all things" by seeking a wife for Isaac. Now the *bakkōl* of all things that are blessed by Yava returns in the Joseph story when the Jacobic frame to the Potiphar's wife episode repeats—four times—that everything Joseph touched was blessed. Not the medieval commentator but Jacob the revisionist picks up on this theme of universal blessing and its relation to fulfillment through children. Jacob is everywhere concerned with generation, and in a sense the blessing of children is his naturalistic counter to Eisaacic piety.

Two general impressions made by the Tamar story encourage us to read it as not simply a contrast to but a reaction against the larger saga that frames it. First, there is the difference in narrative clock. Time passes so quickly, with such relentless concentration on the sequence of birth, sex, and death, that we are impelled to wonder about the abstractness of value so divorced from individuated characters. Related to this is the question of divine or human care in shaping our ends. Nothing is said about whether Judah should or should not have taken Shua for a bedfellow, and nothing is said about the sins of Er, Judah's firstborn. By itself, this kind of narration would be called primitive, and given the choice of which is older, surely most readers would not hesitate to call more ancient, less sophisticated, a story in which Yava slays in a phrase those who displease him over one in which a narrator works out, in the course of several chapters, a scheme of providential justice. But since Onan's spilling of his seed is the one sin that needs to be specified, we are led to regard the narrative style of the episode as ad hoc, created for the purpose of commenting on the larger issues of generation and continuity. Perhaps linguistic history has played an irony at this story's expense in that "onanism" has come to be a synonym for masturbation—an activity at least as innocent as whoring, from the Jacobic perspective. But Onan's sin—Judah's sin—of denying Tamar generational continuity is a sin indeed, or rather a sin of no deed, a sin of omission, reflecting Jacob's interpretation of the Potiphar's wife episode. I do not wish to argue that Jacob's Tamar is to Eisaac's Potiphar's wife as Fielding's Shamela is to Richardson's Pamela; it is not parody that Jacob is about. But just as Fielding's parody restores life in restoring the sexuality slowed out of existence in *Pamela,* so the Tamar story restores, through the concern with generation, a range of human desire and human invention that had too much evaporated from the decorous Eisaacic saga. We might note that Yava is absent from the denouement of the Tamar story because his intervention is no longer needed. He is called upon, in a crude way, to set things going, but Tamar's success proves less a reflection than a Jacobic counter to Eisaacic providence.

What is the relationship between the props and key words of the Tamar story and those related to it in the saga that frames it? There is the goat kid that Judah offers Tamar and the goat the brothers slaughter to dip the coat in blood. There is the recognition theme, with the coat of Joseph and the recognition of the staff, signet, and cord of Judah. There is the whole question of the pledge, the question of pawning one's honor or using one prop, even one child, to "represent" another or a commitment to another. We cannot say the Tamar story "parodies" the story that frames it, for the reaction is not simply a turning against the original; like the *tessera* (the missing piece by which a whole, combined of the broken shards, is recognized), the props within the Tamar story and the story itself stand for the revaluation of the Joseph story, the re-cognition of its themes from the change in context. Perhaps the relation between the Tamar story and the Joseph story can itself be represented by a change in vocabulary within the Tamar story. Judah sleeps with what he takes to be a *zônâ,* a harlot. When Judah sends a surrogate with the goat, the question asked is, "where is that *qĕdēšâ?*"—that cult prostitute. On the one hand, this little face-saving change in term stands as a synecdoche for all the human foible and human energy of self-presentation: Judah wants to look a little better in his surrogate's eye—assuming that visiting a cult prostitute is a step up from visiting a harlot (already a questionable assumption from the standpoint of Eisaacic piety and thus, possibly, a Jacobic joke). But on the other hand, the change from *zônâ* to *qĕdēšâ* is a change transcending character, a change representative of the difference between sexual and spiritual needs. Not "decency" but "story" takes over and turns harlot into devotee, ostensibly profane act into part of a sacred purpose. The Tamar story thus becomes no parody but a re-presentation, a rededication of the narrative that frames it. The progress from a Yava who slays to a Tamar who plans is a minor version of the progress from an old text that decrees to an interpretation that pauses to create new life. Tamar's children, Perez and Zerah, "breakthrough" and "dawning," are the literal new lives representing the triumph of sexuality—of desire, and desire for children—over (Judah's) anxiety about death. This breach-making and coming forth are also synecdoches for midrashic new life—the breakthrough in narrative, the dawning of inspiration when a brilliant Jacob discovers a seminal possibility in an Eisaacic text.

The Question of Lay Analysis

If the will to interpret can be understood as a will to power over a text, we will not be surprised to find that the high achievement of the dream sequences in Genesis chapters 40 and 41 poses particular challenges to Jacob. Often Jacobic revision takes the form of making thematic the relation between older and younger voices. But perhaps nowhere else does the Eisaacic text itself seem so overtly involved in the question of interpretation. We have seen that in the Joseph Saga, the Eisaacic text preempts revisionism to some extent by being all involved with a revisionary theological and literary value: the subtle and slow form of revelation as providence. The distillation of providential solicitude is the prophetic dream, and in these chapters not only dreams but their proper interpretation belong, as Joseph says to the butler and baker, to God (40:8). The first set of dreams shows us that correct interpretation *is* history, proleptically understood. In Pharaoh's court the point is clearer still that anyone can come up with *an* interpretation, but only the interpretation designed—because designated, in advance—for the dreamer will prove to be correct. Thus "designed in advance" and "designed by Eisaac" seem to mean the same thing. Or, to put the point more boldly, the Eisaacic text in proclaiming, "interpretations belong to Elohim," proclaims, "interpretation is preempted by me."

For this reason, chapters 40 and 41—until we get to the actual transfer of power from Pharaoh to Joseph—are, and seemingly "have to be," uninterrupted Eisaacic texts. There is no room for an answering Jacobic voice because these dreams are already answered—in the case of butler and baker by immediate outcome, three days later, and in the case of Pharaoh by the history that follows shortly, the seven years of plenty that Joseph says are nigh upon them. Even when Joseph turns from interpretation proper to words of advice to Pharaoh, "seek out a discerning and wise man and set him over the land of Egypt," the interpretation seems built in. Pharaoh says to his servants, "Could we find anyone better than this [Joseph]—a man filled with the spirit of Elohim?" (41:38). Joseph is already so filled: Interpretation, meaning, spirit fill him in advance of Jacobic revision just as the years of plenty precede the lean years. Lean cow and fat cow are like the belated and original writer: It is not easy to "swallow whole" what is given, especially when it seems so designedly fattened against the ravening maw of revisionism.

When the brothers first appear before Joseph in chapter 42, he accuses them of being spies and devises a test of their truthfulness:

> Thus you shall be tried: If you are true, let one of you brothers be arrested in your "watchhouse" and [the rest of] you go bring home corn for the famine. Then bring back your little brother and your credibility will be established and you shall not die.

What I have done in quoting this passage is to begin with verse 42:15, to skip 15b–18, and to continue with 19–20. The passage coheres, and may represent an original Eisaacic text. The deleted verses add a separate wrinkle:

> "By the life of Pharaoh you won't get out of this unless your little brother comes here! Send one of you to bring your brother, and the rest of you be gathered [hidden] and your words be tested—if the truth is with you—and if not, by Pharaoh's life, you're spies!" Joseph then gathered them to watch [to the "watchhouse"] three days. On the third day, Joseph said, "Do this and live because I fear God. . . ."

Whatever the compositional history of this passage, its theme is a revision in intention for reasons of Eisaacic piety. I have hesitated to translate *mišmār* as "prison house" because the root meaning of "watchfulness" relates the event to the value of being "observant," as Jacob the character was of Joseph's dreams, to see what would happen. Jacob the writer may be similarly "watchful" here, adding a passage of peculiarly Eisaacic sentiment. I do not wish to call Joseph's piety here a parody of Eisaacic religiosity, but it surely represents a more primitive instance than did the speeches of Joseph before butler, baker, and Pharaoh. Joseph "gathers them"—he "Josephs" them into the "house of watchfulness" for three days (the Eisaacic number) in order to repeat, to "add to," to "Joseph" the pattern of bondage and freedom, pit and deliverance, irreverent and pious action. We have no linguistic evidence that this episode is Jacobic, and on the basis of verbal tags a scholar of the documentary hypothesis need not hesitate to label it E material. But if E is not an alternate oral strand but a text available to Jacob to read, master, and imitate in nuance as well as theme, then such a passage may represent the Jacobic reduction of providential to all-too-human designs.

Whether we regard the imprisonment of the brothers as Eisaacic or Jacobic depends on whether we understand Joseph's recantation of the order to hold them all in bondage as a recantation on the part of Joseph himself, or Joseph as he wishes to appear to his brothers, or the narrator who wishes to call attention to what he is doing, what he has decided not to do. If we are thinking of Joseph himself, who first expresses and then modifies a vengeful purpose, then we take at face value Joseph's statement that he "fears God"—that he now fears God, acknowledges the need for moral action, a little more than he did the day before. Yet it is not obvious that the change in plan marks an increase in piety. No hijacker letting go of some of his hostages but leaving his demands unchanged, Joseph implies, rather, that a change in the numbers signifies a change in the meaning of his action. But is that moral meaning (the meaning of one character's motivation within the story) or literary meaning (the meaning of one piece of narrative design when perceived in relation to the rest of the pattern)? Perhaps Joseph's new instruction, "This do and live . . ."—by implying that it is the life of all that is still at stake, that is yet to be redeemed—points to the revised plan as a better re-presentation of the crime, the literary pattern, of single victim, collective good. I believe that the introduction of a first plan and the statement of revised intention are Jacobic midrash, toying with the idea of Joseph as spokesman for Eisaacic piety. The vocabulary is thoroughly Eisaacic, the sentiment ("fears God"), the essence of Eisaacic piety and its relation to moral action; but the self-referentiality of the revision points to another voice: The feel of the phrase suggests Eisaacic material, but the voice is the voice of Jacob. This much is certain: Whether or not the plan to imprison all is actually Jacob's, the episode represents a new power of interpretation, the power of turning Joseph's own will into providential design. Indeed, the very story that shows Joseph proclaiming the fear of God—of what it lies in God's hands to do—reminds us of what it lies in Joseph's hands to do. Reduced to the pit, to a kind of death, to food for worms (there may be a Jacobic pun on *bôr,* "pit," and *bār,* "provender"), Joseph returns, in revised, newly seen, newly feared version, as the "fullness" of God's scheme.

A second minor episode of more clearly Jacobic origin repeats the possibility of mock piety. In the Eisaacic story, the brothers return home, tell Jacob of their conversations and dealings with Joseph, and then empty their sacks—only to find them full of money. What they see (*wayyir'û*) represents what they fear (*wayyîrā'û*). In what appears to be only an additional version of the incident, one added by a redactor who couldn't choose between this revelation and the one in Jacob's presence, the brothers are still on their way home when they encounter their returned money. Several commentators have proposed that their speech there properly belongs later, amid the revelation of the money before Jacob: "What is it that God has done to us?"—especially with the use of

Elohim, not Yava—sounds like Eisaacic material mistakenly transposed to the other version of the incident. (The formula *ʾîš ʾel-ʾaḥîw* [one to another], is also more characteristically E.) But if the incident is a Jacobic reworking of an Eisaacic passage, then the use of Eisaacic phraseology and theology are precisely to the point: Their "heart goes out"—in fear, not sympathy; they turn to one another—in fear, not camaraderie—and wonder what God—not Joseph—has wrought. It is part of the Eisaacic scheme to have the brothers gradually awaken to the reality of providential watchfulness. But it is part of the Jacobic reworking to have readers question whether God's designs or Joseph's machinations are making this emptiness a fullness. Opening their sacks in the Jacobic version, they discover not the shallowness of their moral worth nor the fullness of God's presence but the mere fullness of Joseph's "present" to them. In the mouth of each sack is the money that talks, speaking an ironic kindness that is full of significance but empty of joy. They sold Joseph (at least in the old Eisaacic story) for silver, and here silver returns to haunt them. The Eisaacic God, like their Eisaacic father, silently watches to see the outcome, but the silver in this Jacobic revision speaks and questions the very idea of a judgmental providence packaged in such an easy-open container. The questioning of "silver in the sack" as a signifier for providence may be the meaning—the Jacobic meaning—of having the silver twice discovered.

Beyond the Providence Principle

To understand the place of Jacobic addition at the main climax of the Joseph story—the revelation to the brothers—we must clarify what kind of a climax the story had without Jacobic addition and what possible "motive for meandering" Jacob could have. Linguistic evidence points to an Eisaacic story in which Reuben makes the pathetic offer to his father that Jacob hold Reuben's two sons in pledge: "Slay them if I do not bring [Benjamin back] to you; put [Benjamin] in my hands and I will return him to you" (42:37). The Eisaacic story may then have continued immediately with Jacob's response in 43:13: "Take your brother, return to the man, and Almighty God give you mercy before him that he may release Benjamin and your other brother—and if I am to be bereft—well then, so be it!"

The immediacy of Jacob's response, in such a version, would emphasize his pious resignation. Jacob's thoughts are fixed on Benjamin—a fact that the narrator concisely indicates by having Jacob refer to Simeon as "that other brother"—but he acquiesces to the plan with the thought that what must be, must be. The story might then have proceeded to the scene of the welcome in Joseph's house where Joseph sees Benjamin, cannot contain himself, and reveals himself to the brothers. Two facts about this denouement are exactly right for an Eisaacic tale. First, Joseph spells out the providential design: "God sent me before you to preserve life" (45:5). Second, Joseph releases the brothers from the curse of impeded speech: "And he kissed all his brothers, and wept upon them; and after that they [were able to] talk with him" (45:15). These two climaxes, that of the providential scheme and that of human value, are already there—solemn, sublime, beyond question and beyond forgetfulness.

I have been arguing all along that the relation between the Eisaacic text and the Jacobic voice is too complex for them to be alternative oral strands and too complex for the relation of one to the other to be reduced to mere ironizing. An important weapon, irony remains an *opening* mode, and at this point we are too far advanced, we have too much at stake, to suppose that Jacob can outmaneuver Eisaac with a mere guffaw. One text overgoes the sublime of another not by mocking or dismissing it but by sinking more low to mount more high. I believe we can isolate two such narrative motions in the Jacobic revision. We "sink lower" when the story is slowed for what appear to be unimaginative or extraliterary reasons—the former in the repetition of the hidden treasure motif, the latter in the theme of the Judah-Reuben rivalry. Jacob slows the narrative by having Jacob the character ignore Reuben's offer to pledge his sons. Jacob simply insists, "My son will not go down with you" (42:38). Time passes, food runs out. Meanwhile, the sense of what is involved in this "going down" is deepened. We feel increasingly the identification—through paired alternatives—of Egypt with the grave. To bring Benjamin down to Egypt "is" (is too like) bringing Jacob's old age down to the grave. Benjamin is both the object of focus and the elided object as we pass from the descent of Joseph to the descent of Jacob. The brothers reiterate: The man pestered us with questions about ourselves and our family, asking, "Is your father still alive?" and "Do you have a brother?" And we addressed these concerns. Did we know that he would say, "Bring down your brother!"? (43:7) These lovely, markedly Jacobic lines allow us to see, beyond Benjamin, a perspective opening up from the initial action to the eventual outcome: Do you have a brother? Bring down your brother! Truly, fully to answer the first question or to understand the second is to confront that they have brought down their brother already, and to be ready to confront him anew.

Repetition and originality. In a sense Jacob's challenge is always the same—to make of a retelling the occasion for newness, so that he endlessly renews himself as he renews the challenge to the given text. As we turn to what looks like one of the most unpromising of repetitions—the return of the brothers' food-money—we might stand back for a moment and consider the confrontation between Eisaacic text and Jacobic voice as that between serpent and archetypal man: "He shall bruise your head [your sense of priority], you shall bruise his heel [his *ʿāqēb,* or Jacobic ingenuity]" (3:15). Jacob does seem to be crawling in the dust, chewing over the crumbs and leavings of Eisaacic narrative, when we see Joseph once more telling his steward to fill the brothers' sacks. Yet in a brilliant addition, Jacob has the steward also place Joseph's silver goblet in Benjamin's sack. We have already seen silver suggest the sale of Joseph and the larger moral question about exchange or recompense. Perhaps we can add now that the silver goblet signifies representational power, the power to put forth in miniature, in contained form, something that stands for the lifeblood of the whole story. Most remarkable, most Jacobic, is the specification that this goblet is the one Joseph uses for divination. This is not an easily assimilated detail, and some pious interpreters would have the sentence read, "Behold, this is the one my lord drinks from, and he can divine the evil that you did [in taking it]" (44:5). This seems to accord better with Joseph's own internalization of the power to divine—independent of the cup—in 44:15: "Didn't you know that a person like me can divine?" It's in the person, not the cup. But one has to be piously anticipating or misreading to translate verse 5 thus instead of "Behold, this is the one my lord drinks from—the one he uses *for divining.* You have done evil in what you have done." For the characters within the story, walking off with the magic cup represents no petty thievery but the reduction once again of Joseph's "increase"—a new stripping off of the cloak of special status and a casting down yet once more to the pit of mere mortality. For the narrator, the appearance and disappearance of this special divinatory cup represent the reduction of the providential theme to manipulative magic.

Although Joseph can only feign grievance at the "theft" of so important an object, Jacob the writer knows that there is indeed magic in the cup. It is the linguistic magic of a cup of divination where the word for divining is *lĕnāḥeš,* "to serpent," recalling the archetypal Jacobic challenger ever at the heel. The word also occurs in the dialogue between the wily Laban and the more wily Jacob where Laban says he has "divined" that Jacob is the cause of special blessing (30:27). Perhaps that usage, which follows hard upon the birth of Joseph, suggests a larger Jacobic association of his story of Rachel, stealer of the teraphim, and Joseph's retrieval of the instrument of divination that is the silver cup. Both are sat upon. Although I want to continue to avoid the term "parody," there is always an element of mockery in the Jacobic turn from the divine to divination, from the sublime (God in heaven) to the grotesque (god in the sack). Yet how much more sublime does the story ultimately emerge through this additional midrash on Joseph's "powers of divination"!

The second way Jacob tampers with the climax of the revelation is by inserting Judah's very moving speech between the sight of Benjamin and the uncontrollable tears. Like the story of the stealthily filled sacks, the story of Judah's intervention starts out looking like a reduction of the sublime to a repetition. Yet gradually, the force of re-presenting the "given" as the *oral*, as moving speech, raises Judah to his full height as champion of the Jacobic voice.

The power of Judah's speech on Joseph's ears may be expressed as Jacob's power to repress the individuality of Benjamin as distinct from Joseph and more immediately the object of concern. Judah first answers Joseph:

> What shall we say to my lord? How shall we speak? And how shall we be justified? God has found out your servants' iniquity. Behold—we are your lordship's servants—all of us, [not just] him in whose hand the cup is found.

Joseph then insists on isolating the one from the group—perhaps poignantly insisting on the very mode of individuation that Reuben and Judah had to address when the brothers conspired against Joseph: "Far be it from me to do that sort of thing: The one in whose hand the goblet is found—he, he shall be my servant, and the rest of you can go in peace to your father!"

Judah's reply now specifies, for the first time in their exchange, that Benjamin is one of two absent brothers, the other being dead. In repeating Joseph's demands and Jacob's response, Judah not only humbles himself before the force of Jacob's pathos, but forces Joseph to confront the overwhelming reality and separateness of Jacob's affection for Benjamin:

> "The one went out from me, and I said, 'Surely a wild beast has devoured him'—and I haven't seen him since. And you would take this one too from my face—and if an accident should befall him, you would bring my old age in evil to the grave." And now—if I come to your servant my father and the boy is not—his soul is tied to his soul.

One is immediately led to supply the missing antecedents for the pronouns: Jacob's soul is bound to Benjamin's soul, so that Jacob will "read" Benjamin's absence as Jacob's "absence" and die. But the added pathos of *napšô qĕšûrâ bĕnapsô*—soul bound to soul without specification of pronouns—is that Joseph must confront the sublimity of an affection of which he is both present force (since the absence of Joseph has intensified the bond to Benjamin) and irrelevant other: it is Jacob's love *for Benjamin* that is now a matter of life and death.

Benjamin either way is the "watershed" between dissembling and tears.

But in the Eisaacic account, the sheer presence of Benjamin standing before him is too much for Joseph, while in the extraordinary Jacobic addition, *Judah's speech,* Judah's re-presentation of Benjamin as Jacob's love and "lifeline," sink Joseph into pathos and raise the scene to new sublimity.

Jitneys and Their Relation to the Unconscious

Whatever the problems in expressing happiness in experience, there is a special literary problem—call it a "happy problem"—about how to translate an emotion into visible, enumerable signs of affection or joy. Sometimes gifts are given whose symbolic number stands for the spiritual presence one can hardly measure by measuring the gifts themselves—seven wells or seven daughters, for example. Sometimes the specification of great number has to stand for great emotion: Esau receives two hundred she goats and twenty he goats, two hundred ewes and twenty rams. Some narratives seem themselves to be raising the question about the problem of translation into number or visible sign; in others, a character voices the query: "Why do I need all this?" or "Why did you send so thick?" Joseph's lavish present to Jacob raises the old question in a welcome context, and perhaps there is a subtle Eisaacic joke built into the tale of Jacob's reception of the news of Joseph being still alive—translated into Jacob's reception of the laden asses and ready wagons. "Jacob's heart was faint because he did not believe [the brothers with their good news]. They told him everything Joseph said; but when he saw the wagons that Joseph sent to carry him back, the spirit of Jacob their father revived" (45:26–27). "If he sent the limousine, he must be alive." Or maybe, "If he sent the limo with the extra luggage rack, he must be my son, for only my son would remember how much baggage I carry when I have to travel." A lovely passage in Midrash Rabba stands as evidence that the text poses a problem about the special importance of those wagons to Jacob's emotional state. Jacob saw in "wagon" (*ʿăgālâ*) a pun on heifer (*ʿeglâ,* spelled with the same Hebrew letters) and said to himself—Joseph and I were studying the the section of the Talmud on the laws of the red heifer at the time of Joseph's disappearance; only Joseph would have known what we were discussing—it must be Joseph! The charm of this midrash comes in part from the appropriateness of an anachronism at just this juncture: A Joseph who is yet alive seems no less a miracle than a talmudic debate already extant at the time of Jacob. But the midrash also, and less abstractly, converts the physical gift into spiritual bond: Not wagons, but subjects of study, occasions for father-son, teacher-student dialogue.

If such a midrashic occasion were perceived by Jacob confronting the

Eisaacic text, he may have expatiated in a similar vein in two responses to Jacob's Eisaacic "revival." First, there is the line spoken by Jacob the character at this point: "It is enough; Joseph my son is still alive; I will go and see him before I die" (45:28). Idiomatic expression, and perhaps most startlingly the shift to the name "Israel" rather than "Jacob" at this point, have made scholars inclined to identify the line as a contribution from the J source. If it represents a Jacobic reaction to what we have just heard—that Father Jacob's heart revived on seeing the wagons—then the *rab* (it is enough) represents a specifically midrashic response to an old text: "Enough wagons." Life has riches enough if there is time granted me to see Joseph before I die. The beautiful question that has haunted the Eisaacic tale, *haʿôd ʾabî ḥāy* (Is my father yet alive?) returns as assertion: *ʿôd yôsēp bĕnî ḥāy* (Joseph my son is yet alive!). In such a return, we are beyond five changes of raiment, thirty pieces of silver, ten laden asses, or whatever enumerable recompenses may have occurred to the old teller of the tale. If this line is indeed Jacobic writing, then it comments not only on the narrative that precedes it but on the episode that follows, the peculiarly Eisaacic return to direct revelation of Elohim telling Jacob not to fear to descend to Egypt. The Jacobic *ʾerʾennû* (I'll go see him!) preempts the Eisaacic half-pun on sight and fear, as well as the dignified Eisaacic prophecy that Joseph will close the eyes of Jacob when he finally dies.

The second Jacobic midrash on *ʿăgālôt* present not in Genesis Rabba but already in Genesis itself comes when Jacob arrives in Goshen. Now Joseph prepares his own chariot—again, a gesture especially full of meaning if it is a later author's response to an earlier one's chariots sent in absentia. Now the word *ʿôd* (still) doubly draws out the time: Joseph falls on Jacob's neck and weeps over him; the embrace lasts *ʿôd* (it is still going on, or "he wept over his neck a good while," as a decorous translation has it). Then Jacob repeats to Joseph his expression of happiness as the exchangeability of this moment for all time: "I will die [I would fain die, I would be willing to go to my grave thinking, 'it is enough, it is well'] now that I have seen your face" (46:30). In substituting human value for divine revelation, this verse recalls Jacob's sentiment upon meeting Esau. But the verbal echoes are much closer: We bring up from the recent narrative past Joseph's query, "Is my father still alive?"—but we bring up from the more recent past Jacob's realization, before he traveled to Egypt, "Joseph, my son, is yet alive" (45:28). The simple change from third person to second sums up all the father's emotion with magnificent declarative: "*you are yet alive!*"

Joseph's verbal response punctuates the emotional fullness of the scene by appearing to break off: *ʾeʿĕleh wĕʾaggîdâ lĕparʿōh* (I'll go up and tell Pharaoh . . .). In part, this turn to other matters functions to isolate and leave holy the beautiful encounter in which the single verbal turn from question (Is my father yet alive?) to happy declarative (You are still alive!) is sufficient and more than sufficient. The scene is especially glorious because it lacks Joseph's emotive words to Jacob, much like a scene of reunited family in which care is expressed by the inability to express anything except "I'll go look after the soup." When the inside is so full, one can only turn "outside." Yet the repetition of *'eʿĕleh* (I will go up) frames the scene in a way that adds a further perfection: Joseph goes up to Jacob, he goes up to Pharaoh to show (the Hebrew in 46:28 is *lĕhôrōt,* to show the way, to "parent") what true return means. In the Eisaacic text Joseph declares that he has been made a "father to Pharaoh" (45:8), but the Jacobic midrash finds more power in humility, more sublimity in the self-limitation, more spirituality in the sublimation of a power struggle into filial homage.

The Future of a Confusion

Two rich scenes of benediction conclude the Eisaacic narrative. In one, Jacob encounters Pharaoh and there is a moment when all the weight of years, all the burdens of experience, seem lifted simply by being acknowledged as objective fact, something from which the two fathers of their people stand aside: "Few and evil have been the days of my life; they have not attained to the days of my fathers" (47:9). How long have I lived, you ask? Not much. A hundred and thirty years. It's been short and rotten. Whether or not there is delicate humor in this scene, there is about it a dignity untouchable by Jacobic thoughts, and we turn to the second scene, Jacob's blessing of Joseph's children. Here too there is extraordinary delicacy, but not perhaps the same sense of taboo about tinkering with the text. We may suppose that the Eisaacic narrative was originally contiguous as Joseph brings Ephraim and Menasseh to Jacob and Jacob blesses them: First Jacob speaks of them in absentia as adopted sons: "Ephraim and Menasseh, like Reuben and Simeon, shall be mine" (48:5). He then asks Joseph to call the children to him, and Joseph does so.

> He brought them close to [Jacob] and [Jacob] kissed and hugged them. Israel said, "I had not thought to see your face—and behold, Elohim has shown me also your seed!" He blessed them that day, saying, "In you shall Israel bless, saying, 'Elohim make you like Ephraim and Menasseh!'"

I have quoted 48:10–11, 20 as though the text were continuous. What would make someone notice—or create—a space for interpretation in such a text? If the Eisaacic narrative already included the phrase "Ephraim and Menasseh," as in verse 20, a reader might notice the minor priority of Ephraim over Menasseh simply in Ephraim's being mentioned first—and decide to make something of it. Perhaps the entirety of verse 20, which continues, "and he set Ephraim before Menasseh," was already given. In any case, Jacob the writer has history on his side, history that has shown Ephraim to be the more important tribe, perhaps *the* tribe for Eisaac. I do not mean to imply that Eisaac was writing prophecy and Jacob history; both writers are looking back at mythical origins of historical facts. But only Jacob looks back with a secular glance, in at least the root meaning of "secular": full of the knowledge of the years, understanding that Yava declares his nature to be *ʾehyeh ʾăšer ʾehyeh* (I will be that which will be); God reveals himself in passing, so that only his "hinderparts," only the "afterglow" or "aftermeditation" of events shows his glory. More precisely, what the passing years bring, for Jacob, is the understanding that what will be, will be: Not God *will be,* but history *has been.* The same story-facts thus mean differently for Eisaac and Jacob. For Eisaac, the prophecy about Ephraim's priority is just that—prophetic utterance, speech filled with what feels like supernatural, or at least farsighted, wisdom. For Jacob, the priority of Ephraim might be called an irony—the irony that Eisaacic "providence," when the mist is past, turns out to be ordinary hindsight. But irony is the wrong term, for Jacob's motive is not demystification but transumption—the acquisition of power from understanding the "early" as "late."

To effect—and represent—this transumption, Jacob lingers over this lovely scene of the blessing, projecting Eisaacic piety onto Joseph and introjecting Jacobic wiliness—the wisdom of Jacob the character as the strategy of Jacob the writer. In the Jacobic account, it is Joseph who now represents Eisaac both in the desire to be himself blessed and in the desire to "get it right" about Ephraim and Menasseh:

> Joseph saw that his father set his right hand on the head of Ephraim, and this looked bad to him; he held his father's hand to remove it from the head of Ephraim to the head of Menasseh. Joseph said to his father, "Not so, my father, for this one is the firstborn! Put your right [hand] on his head." But his father declined and said, "I know, my son, I know: he too will be a people and he too will be great, but his little brother will be greater. . . ." (48:17–19)

Jacob's gentle acknowledgement, *yādaʿtî bĕnî yādaʿtî* (I know, my son, I know) may include a pun, or at least a suggestion, of the *yad,* the hand that has been a motif throughout the story and a locus of the ambiguity about providence: Are the events as they turn out indicative of the hand of Joseph (his sway, his control, as in 39:22) or the "hand of God" (a phrase characteristic of the Exodus story, but one that may be used to represent the providential theme throughout the Joseph story)? The brothers who want to keep their hands clean (37:22, 27) and who wish to have Benjamin entrusted into their hands (42:37, 43:9) know not their right from their left. Even Benjamin, who is found with the goblet "in hand," as it were, in 44:17, is blind to the shaping hand of what Eisaac calls God, what Jacob may ultimately regard as the narrator. But dim-eyed Jacob the character can see very well because, in the words of Shakespeare's Gloucester, "I see it feelingly": By embracing Ephraim and Menasseh, Jacob embraces his grandchildren as his children; he embraces likewise history as providence. Jacob the narrator introjects the power of benediction, the power that had been that of being privileged, being at the knees of the father bestowing the efficacious blessing. As the story winds to a close, Joseph, who fears God, who knows that he is not in "place of God" (50:19) remains behind to repeat, in dignified but muffled tones, something of the Jacobic patience. But it is an Eisaacic Joseph we see breathing his last in Genesis 50. Jacob the narrator dies with the death of Jacob the character, and he dies leaving us with the monumental impression of his being father, precursor of Joseph—of Eisaacic Joseph, *of Eisaac,* as it were. Perhaps it is no accident that the last line that scholars of the documentary hypothesis have attributed to "J" should sound so much the tone of Eisaacic piety, even while proclaiming the theme of the land so dear to the heart of J: "Joseph said to his brothers, 'I die, and Elohim will surely visit you and bring you up from this land to the land promised to Abraham, Isaac, and Jacob'" (50:24). To make the documentary sources come out right, scholars need to suppose an editorial substitution of *Elohim* for *Yava.* But if the line is written by a revisionist Jacob, there is no need to suppose such a tinkering. Jacob leaves us with a vision of Eisaacic Joseph prophesying divine presence, and repeating in a finer (thinner, weaker) tone the Jacobic tie to Canaan. Elohim *will be* present, but Yava already has been alive and well in tales that come not after Genesis but in it, mixing with and challenging the priority of the old, Eisaacic narrative. The Eisaacic text goes on to frame the story, now that the voice of Jacob is past. In Genesis, the last original gesture of Jacob, genius of belatedness, is this "transumption" or self-transformation into the prevenient spirit of human care.

ACKNOWLEDGMENTS

I would like to own the help I have received from Moshe Greenberg and Brevard Childs. Nothing in their venerable publications, inspiring seminars, or generous conversation suggested special tolerance for the perspective I have taken in this book, and my gratitude to them should in no way be taken as an intimation of their endorsement. Marc Brettler's magnanimous suspension of disbelief in this project let me dream that in a world to come, as in some world gone by, Jacobic spirits could sit and share midrashim on old, Eisaacic tales. Herbert Marks and James W. Watts stretched out mighty arms to save me from drowning in a sea of earlier drafts' errors. And to Harold Bloom, Genius of the Shore: I acknowledge all the good of thy large influence, however accompanied by sad dismay at my wandering in too normative a flood.

On a visit to the mid-Hudson Hebrew Day School some years ago, I heard an eight-year-old boy deliver, in faltering Hebrew, a most unfaltering version of Abraham's response to a voice that called for the sacrifice of Isaac. Although the assignment was to supply the missing conversation between Abraham and God, this uncooperative student insisted that Abraham said not a word. The boy had certainly not read the Book of Jubilees, but he knew a Mastima when he heard one, and he had Abraham respond with the speedy and silent sacrifice of—his ass. I want to thank that boy for keeping alive my faith that we live not in an age too late to hear and revere, in the likes of his still small voice, the voice of Jacob.

WORKS CITED

The following is strictly a list of works cited rather than a core reading list. More extensive bibliography can be found in a number of works named here, especially that of Gordon Wenham.

Alter, Robert. *The Art of Biblical Narrative.* New York: Basic Books, 1981.

Carpenter, J. Estlin, and G. Harford-Battersby. *The Hexateuch . . . Arranged in Its Constituent Documents.* London: Longmans, Green, and Co., 1900. 2 vols.

Sandmel, Samuel. "The Haggada within Scripture." *Journal of Biblical Literature* 80 (1961): 105–22.

Speiser, E. A. *Genesis.* The Anchor Bible. Garden City, N.Y.: Doubleday, 1964.

Van Seters, John. *Abraham in History and Tradition.* New Haven: Yale University Press, 1975.

Von Rad, Gerhard. *Genesis: A Commentary.* The Old Testament Library. Trans. John H. Marks. Philadelphia: The Westminster Press, 1972.

Wellhausen, Julius. *Prolegomena to the History of Ancient Israel.* Trans. Menzies and Black. Cleveland: World Publishing, 1957.

Wenham, Gordon J. *Genesis 1–15.* Word Biblical Commentary. Waco, Texas: Word Books, 1987.

Westermann, Claus. *Genesis 1–11: A Commentary; 12–36* [vol. II]; *37–50* [vol. III]. Trans. John J. Scullion. Minneapolis: Augsburg Publishing House, 1984, 1985, 1986.